The Chamberlain Negotiation Principles

The Chamberlain Negotiation Principles

A Tale of Five Must Know
Negotiation Tenets
and the Insight
Behind the Principles
to Help You Succeed

Jared Kelner

Title: The Chamberlain Negotiation Principles

Subtitle: A Tale of Five Must Know Negotiation
Tenets and the Insight Behind the Principles to
Help You Succeed

Publisher: The Infinite Mind Training Group
PO Box 25, East Brunswick, NJ 08816-0025

Author: Jared Kelner

Editor: Cynthia Willett Sherwood
    Second Set of Eyes (www.secondsetofeyes.com)

Cover Art: Wicked Sunny
    Publishing Gurus (www.publishinggurus.com)

ISBN - 10: 0982655800
ISBN - 13: 9780982655801

First Edition, 2010

Published in the United States of America

To Debbie, for always lighting up the room

Table of Contents

Introduction

What is the definition of a negotiation? Consider that question seriously for a few moments. To get the most out of this book, it is important that you challenge yourself to think about negotiations from a new perspective. Setting aside the negotiations people have with themselves in their own minds, most would say that a negotiation consists of at least two people with different demands, objectives, or positions who are working to create an agreement—sometimes friendly, but sometimes hostile—over something one of the parties has control over that the other party wants. This definition could be debated for years, and that debate is a negotiation of sorts, but the concept of creating a definition of a negotiation that the general public would accept is relatively simple. Unfortunately, when we try to define negotiations intellectually, we leave out a critical element that dramatically impacts the outcome of the negotiation. That missing piece is the human element. In order to master the art of negotiating, you must always remember that you are interacting with someone very much like yourself: a living, breathing person with thoughts, feelings, biases, and motivations. It is from this starting point that *The Chamberlain Negotiation Principles* was written.

Whether in business or in your personal life, regardless of what is being negotiated and by whom, every single negotiation has some element of human emotion. It is human nature to feel emotions as you jockey for position, counter an objection with a well thought out argument, realize you've been swindled, or create a mutually agreeable contract from which both sides benefit. Any negotiation book worth its weight offers proven techniques, theories, or exercises to help people better understand this complex process, validates what novices and experts know or at the very least challenges individuals to look at the topic from a different angle. But often times, critical information that could help people succeed in their next negotiation is lost inside the pages if the examples and explanations are presented in a dry, textbook style. Here is where *The Chamberlain Negotiation Principles* offers something unique. *The Chamberlain Negotiation Principles* combines the literary genres of fiction and nonfiction into one book by weaving important negotiation tenets through a poignant story that casts a light upon the human element of negotiations and also offers in-depth academic analysis of the negotiation principles shared in the fable to ensure a comprehensive understanding of the process. The result is an entertaining and valuable negotiation resource that will touch your heart and challenge your mind.

Prologue

Disaster struck Chamberlain Zacharias Taylor III in the winter of 1958. Without warning, the conveyor belts halted and were frozen in time. Young Chamberlain stood at his office window overlooking the factory that his grandfather built with his powerful hands. The sudden passing of his father left the 28-year-old Chamberlain in charge of the business, a responsibility for which he knew he was not prepared. Chamberlain pressed his forehead shamefully against the glass, and prayed he'd shatter it and his existence together with one violent thrust. Time stood as still as the devastated workers. With the exception of the occasional mouse that crept across the cold concrete floor, nothing moved. How could a thriving textile factory that supplied 8 percent of the United States' clothing manufacturers fall victim to bankruptcy? What had Chamberlain done to his grandfather's and father's dream? He had killed it. That's exactly what he had done. The factory was one of the first African American owned businesses in Charlotte, and the community blamed Chamberlain for destroying it. Everyone believed he had killed the family business with his arrogance, his immaturity, and his unwillingness to listen to his elders—not to mention his drinking and gambling. Fifty years and three generations of service were poured into this factory, and there was no question in anyone's mind that it was

Chamberlain Zacharias Taylor III who cut the heart out of the business. He alone was responsible for the lost wages of the 613 citizens of North Carolina who desperately needed this factory for their survival, but it was unsalvageable. Mistake after mistake after mistake created a devastating mudslide that buried everything in its path.

Chamberlain returned to his desk and opened his leather journal. Today's entry would be his last, and Chamberlain swore to himself that when he finished writing, he would never speak about this moment again. He took the pen from the desk and began to write.

January 26, 1958

Poppa, I forgive you. I promise that I will carry the truth to my grave and I will never let them know what you did to Grandpa's dream. Let them believe it was me. Let them all blame me for this devastation so you will be remembered with love. I miss you so much. Why did you have to die so young? There was so much more for me to learn from you. You left me too soon. I was too young to take over and everyone knew it. I was not ready to lead these people, but what choice did I have? I tried my best to fix it all, Poppa. I tried to set things right, but you left me alone with all of your mistakes. I gambled to try to fix things, but I failed, Poppa. None of that matters now. I am to blame. Let them believe it was me. I miss you. I love you, Poppa.

Chamberlain locked the journal and the truth it held inside his desk drawer, then carefully wrapped the key inside his handkerchief and dropped the cloth into the wastebasket. He grabbed the bottle of whiskey from the desk and drank until it was empty. At 2:00 a.m., long after everyone had uselessly clocked out for the last time, Chamberlain closed the office door that his grandfather and father before him had walked through thousands of times, and slowly descended the wooden stairs. He had never paid attention to the look and feel of the polished brass handrail that ran the entire length of the staircase, but as he borrowed its strength to steady himself step after step, he bowed his head in sorrow and prayer. Chamberlain paused at the bottom of the stairs and looked up to the heavens where he knew his ancestors were gazing down upon him. A single tear hit the floor, and he quietly said, "Forgive me."

That was the last anyone in Charlotte saw or heard from Chamberlain Zacharias Taylor III. He disappeared, never to return to his home or to his family. His wife and young daughter wept for weeks, but eventually learned to survive on their own. They never stopped wondering how he could just leave. What kind of a man had Chamberlain become to abandon his family? Where did he go? Was he still alive? Would they ever see him again?

Chapter 1

Richard was exhausted. He exhaled for the first time in two days as he sat on the splintered wooden steps just outside the withered Calvary Baptist Church. His watch read 4:55 p.m. January 25, 2010. The evening brought a chill to the stale air that had enveloped him all day. Richard had arrived in Charlotte, North Carolina only a few hours before and could not begin to wrap his heart and mind around the events of the last seven weeks that brought him to this distant soil. His eyes darted across the parking lot in front of him, trying to focus on something to help settle his heart, but the scenery offered nothing in return, so Richard breathed slowly and allowed his knotted muscles to finally relax, as he simply thought about Chamberlain.

How could one man that he had known for such a short time so quickly become the foundation upon which he would build his life? Richard knew in his gut he would never be the same again. He knew that he was young and green and that most 22-year-old men would not have been ready to understand the advice Chamberlain imparted to him, but Richard was not most young men, at least not anymore.

He loosened his tie, rolled up his sleeves, and realized, for the first time in years, that he was going to be fine. Better than fine. He was going to be content in life. He was going to be successful in life. He wasn't truly sure what that meant—to be successful in life—

but a feeling of hope swept over him. He smiled and just knew.

Cherise tiptoed up behind Richard, but the groaning of the weather-beaten floorboards announced her approach. She placed her hand on Richard's head and patted it like her grandma had done for years. She wore her faded white Sunday church dress, which had been handed down from her cousin, but Cherise cared for it, mended it, washed it, and always wore it with love. She knew that she looked adorable in it. Tiny ribbons of yellow and green spotted her tight corn rows, and at that moment, she was the sweetest seven-year-old girl in all of North Carolina, a fact that no one could deny. As her hand rustled Richard's hair, she said, "Everyone inside is crying, sir. You made a whole lot of people sad in there. They're all just sitting, crying and thinking, about my great-grandpa."

Richard sighed and said, "I'm so sorry, sweetheart. I didn't mean for that to happen. I just wanted your family to know what a wonderful man he was and how much respect I have for him."

"That's the thing, sir. No one inside knew him like you did. All I've ever known about him are the stories they tell about a young man who ruined the family business and then left his family, but the way you talk about him, I don't see how he could have done all the things they said he did."

"What's your name?"

"Cherise, sir. My grandma is Chamberlain's daughter."

"Well, Cherise, your great-grandfather was a special man, and I don't believe he did all those bad things. I read the newspaper article. I know what they said about him, but there is more to it than people know. The Chamberlain I knew would not have destroyed his family or his business the way they say he did. So we just have to believe he was a good man that moved on to a better place."

"You're a good man, Mr. Richard. My grandma called you a blessing."

Richard smiled. He never thought of himself as anything more than a regular guy, but if befriending Chamberlain made him a blessing, he would humbly accept the honor.

"Cherise, I believe Chamberlain was a good man too. I will carry him with me the rest of my life, and I hope you'll do the same."

"Mr. Richard, would you mind telling me the whole story? But this time, please tell me everything that happened between you and my great-grandpa. All I know is that he did bad things to the family and to the people down here. I want to know what he was really like, and I get the feeling that you knew him better than anyone."

Richard gazed into the child's deep brown eyes and was overcome with a sense of love, of family, and of pain. He let the evening air fill his lungs and exhaled slowly to prepare himself to relive the events that had unfolded over the last few weeks. Richard put his arm around Cherise and said, "I guess we should start at the beginning."

Chapter 2

Nearly all of Richard's friends who graduated with him from the business school at Ohio State University were recruited to large companies as sales reps, business development managers, product managers, and other lofty titles, but Richard, for all his talents, cum laude grades, youthful eagerness, and movie star good looks, was left behind and did not find work right out of school. He was an aggressive and qualified candidate for any company that would have him, so this setback was not about to stop Richard from starting his career.

After researching the job markets across America, Richard determined that Manhattan, with its vast array of business opportunities, was the best place to live if you were a 22-year-old unemployed college graduate in pursuit of a career in sales, so he stuffed his ego into his backpack, jumped into a taxi, and headed to the airport.

The flight was uneventful, which he realized, with all the insanity and in-flight terror of the past decade, was the best kind of flight possible. After landing and retrieving his bags from the luggage carousel, he hailed a cab and headed to his new home: a musty one-bedroom apartment in SoHo. It had less style and even fewer amenities than his college dorm room, but Richard was grateful for his parents' offer to cover his rent for six months while he tried to find a job. However, if he failed to make it on his own, his future would be decided for him. Richard recalled the last thing his father said before he left Ohio:

"We'll pay for your rent for six months, but not one day more. We've sunk too much into your education to abandon you now, but you better get off your butt and land yourself a job or we're going to find one for you. Do you understand?"

And he did understand. He understood all too well what it meant when his folks said they'd find him a job. It meant coming back home to central Jersey, a failure in his mind, to work as an assistant manager at his father's convenience store selling generic brand foods to the local boring community. He'd grown up in that store, restocking, sweeping the floors, cleaning the bathrooms, and working the register; the last place he wanted to be was wearing that embarrassing white apron, with a price gun in his pocket, walking the aisles of that dead-end store. Richard knew in his heart that he was destined for more, and he had no intention of considering that life before he gave a real run at creating his own future. Richard loved and respected his parents for providing for the family and for paying for his education, but he couldn't imagine a life spending his days selling low-end knock-off food to unappreciative customers from six o'clock in the morning to eleven o'clock at night, seven days a week. It just wasn't the life Richard envisioned for himself, and he was not going to settle for it.

Chapter 3

The first stop for Richard after he dumped his bags, showered, shaved, and hand ironed the deep creases in his charcoal-colored suit, was to the local temp agency to begin the journey of discovering who he was meant to be, or at least to find a job.

A tiny metal bell above the threshold jingled a few times as the door swung open. The sound was supposed to alert the temp agency staff that a new client had just walked in, but not a single employee looked up to acknowledge the bell or Richard. He froze for a moment and contemplated leaving to look for another temp agency—one that would greet him with enthusiasm. But time was not on his side, so he settled himself and walked directly to the heavy-set man behind the old wooden desk.

He had never seen an obese man with a prominent Adam's apple, but somehow, Bruce was blessed with a walnut-sized nugget right in the middle of his bloated neck. According to the plastic nameplate on his desk, Bruce had no last name. When he finally looked up at Richard, he simply said, "Resume."

Richard extended a manila envelope to Bruce. Inside the pouch was supposed to be his ticket to a better life, but all Bruce could say after glancing at Richard's credentials was, "Buckeye, huh?"

Richard noticed the coffee-stained Michigan mug sitting on Bruce's desk, but chose not to take the college rivalry bait. He politely smiled, but kept his mouth shut. His mind was focused on avoiding the family convenience store at all cost, even if it meant kissing up to the portly Wolverine. As Bruce clumsily multitasked between a slice of sausage pizza and his computer keyboard, he stared blankly at the resume and said, "So, what kind of work are you looking for, Richard Cast?"

"Ideally, I would like something in sales, but if you can find me a good company to work for, I'd be willing to consider other opportunities."

"How much are you looking to make per hour?"

"My target is between $20 and $25."

"Per hour?!?! Come on now, kid. Get serious. You've got no experience. You're fresh out of school so every employer knows that you'll take anything they offer. Let's try this again. How much per hour?"

Richard felt his body sink into the stiff wooden chair. He felt defeated, but knew the alternatives, so he manufactured another smile, and said, "Bruce, just find me a job, please."

The two men sat in silence for fifteen minutes as Bruce pounded away at the crumbling keyboard and inconsiderately backed Richard's future into a range of "no less than $12, no more than $18 per hour." A printer kicked on next to Bruce, and the ancient dot matrix unit scratched out Richard's first assignment as a $12 per hour telemarketer selling frozen meat, fish, and poultry shipped in from Colorado.

With that, Richard stood, folded the perforated page into quarters, tucked it into his breast pocket, thanked the man with no last name, and listened to the bell above the door jingle once more as he wilted onto the sidewalk. He thought to himself, *"What the hell did I just do? $12 to $18 per hour? I'm better than this!"* The strangers that passed by stared at him as if he was one of those crazy guys who talk to themselves all day long about garbage or the war or a lost shoe, and he realized that he had been thinking out loud. He knew the passers-by were justified in thinking he was a bum because that was exactly how he felt, like a bum on the street with nowhere to call home.

Chapter 4

It was now the fifth month of his career search and his parental-enforced six month deadline was fast approaching. Richard was a miserable employee on his fourth assignment, and the previous three jobs were only somewhat less ridiculous. He was insulted by the offers and even more disgusted with himself that he accepted the petty terms. "No less than $12, no more than $18 per hour" was a crock. He'd earned no less than $12, but also no more than $12. He'd earned $12 per hour at the last three jobs, and there was no possibility he'd survive through the month. Thoughts of the family convenience store now actually seemed less painful, less shameful than suffering through another temp job with Bruce as his backer. What had he become? How could such a smart, talented, attractive, and energetic young man have fallen so far from his potential in such a short amount of time? His hopes of landing that perfect temp job, knocking it out of the park and being asked to come on board as a full-time employee with benefits, a cell phone allowance, and a laptop were all but a distant dream. Richard was coming to the realization that he was walking the plank and stood less than two weeks from jumping overboard and falling into an ocean full of generic chocolate chip cookies and processed bologna.

One Monday morning, while on his way to the local copy shop—his most recent $12 per hour assignment—Richard found himself on 8th Avenue and 34th Street staring up at a high-rise office building. Out of nowhere, twenty perfectly groomed young professionals in pressed suits approached him from behind like a battalion in formation. The stampede was headed straight for the revolving door behind him, and without any time to sidestep the pack, Richard got swept up in their undercurrent and was forced inside the building. He tried to break free, but before he had time to turn around, he was pushed inside the elevator like a sardine. As the doors closed, everyone fell silent and listened to the Musak version of Survivor's *Eye of the Tiger*. All of the young professionals faced forward, checked their breath, popped mints, and picked lint from their clothes. Richard was facing backward and had no room to turn around, so he closed his eyes and went along for the ride up to the eleventh floor.

Richard planted his feet firmly as the bell chimed and the doors opened. Pushing their way past Richard, the crowd piled out of the elevator and headed for the office at the end of the hallway. Richard turned and placed a hand on the elevator door to stop it from closing as he watched the scene. *Where was he? Who were these people? Where were they going? Should he join them? Should he leave? If he left, where would he go? Back home to face his parents? No.* He was not ready to admit defeat. How could he not succeed after all the money his parents invested in his university education and city housing? He knew exactly how his parents would react, but why bother replaying that story in his head? Something had to change now or his future would be run over by cases of spray-can cheese and single-ply no-name toilet paper.

As the elevator door closed behind Richard, the last of the young professionals walked into the lobby of a business called X-Ray Query, LLC. It was now or never, so Richard sprinted down the hallway and caught the door just before it closed. He stepped inside as inconspicuously as possible and followed the crowd into a small conference room. The twenty-by-twenty room had two large windows that overlooked 34th Street, five long conference tables arranged neatly in rows, a solid oak lectern at the front and a metal framed mirror on the side wall. He took a seat in the back row and tried to blend in. Realizing that he was the only one in the room not dressed in a suit, he quickly created his phantom excuse about the lint fire at the dry cleaners that had damaged all his professional clothes. He grabbed a pen from his pocket, placed Bruce's latest assignment sheet upside down onto the table in front of him, and waited in silence along with the rest of the hopeful young professionals.

With an immediate sense of power and control, Dr. Alan Branch entered the conference room. The doctor was barely 29 when he sold his first bio-medical research company for $18.5 million dollars. He was 34-

years-old now, and prior to starting X-Ray Query, LLC, Dr. Branch had created and then quickly sold two additional medical research companies. He was a lion among mice. Mentally, he could out-maneuver the sharpest minds of the day. From a business perspective, he had a knack for predicting market trends and possessed an innate ability to control the destiny of his companies. He stood 6' 2" tall with broad shoulders and looked like he could have been the adult love child of Robert Redford and Sophia Loren.

But for all of Dr. Branch's accomplishments, Richard had no clue who had just entered the room. Dr. Branch could have been some out-of-work Broadway actor on a temp assignment coming to talk to a group of intellectuals about how to dress for success. So Richard sat quietly and waited for things to unfold. Dr. Branch took the front of the room and began with precision.

"Good morning and welcome to your future. I am Dr. Alan Branch, the founder and CEO of X-Ray Query, LLC. You have been hand selected to be my voice and evangelists to the medical masses. My hope is that the education you'll receive throughout your training here will help you all become skilled negotiators. My objective with this business, as it was for my previous three, is to develop a market demand for our specialized technology, grow the revenue to millions of dollars per year, and then sell the company to the highest bidder. You will quickly learn that I am a focused individual and that I do not waste any time or energy with distractions that pull me away from my objectives. Please never take anything personal here. It is all about building revenue and creating a market demand. Do not expect us to become friends. I am your CEO and as such, I expect you to address me accordingly. My interest in you is strictly professional. What you should expect is that you will be well trained, and if you succeed, you will be compensated quite fairly. My expectations of you are simple. Prepare each day. Work smart all the time. And sell, sell, sell."

Dr. Branch pointed to a mountain of paperwork on the front table and then landed his gaze upon a young man sitting eagerly in the front row.

"You there. Please hand a welcome packet to every person in the room."

The eager recruit immediately complied. Bursting from his seat, he scooped up the papers and leaped around the room like a trained kangaroo, ensuring that each binder found its new master. Richard did not make eye contact with the recruit when the paperwork was dropped on the table in front of him. He simply placed both hands on top of it, as if to claim the file for himself and no one else. When the young man finished handing out the packets, he returned to his seat and was about to proudly sit down, but stopped dead in his tracks, this time like a kangaroo in the wild that had come face to face with an Outback hunter's rifle. With his back to Dr. Branch, he stared at his empty desk only to discover that in his haste to please the boss, he forgot to give himself a packet, and unfortunately, there were no more. He was unsure of what to do next, so he slowly turned to face the medical mogul. Without hesitation, Dr. Alan Branch spoke.

"Thank you. Seeing that you are without a training manual, you may leave now."

The entire room fell silent. Richard thought to himself, *"Could he be serious? Could this madman actually be firing this guy before he had even begun the race? Did I just pick-pocket a job from a total stranger? Should I speak up? I shouldn't be here. I stole his future."* Before he could utter a word, the young man ran out of the room like a wounded marsupial, leaving his future on Richard's desk.

Everyone was in shock. No one knew what to do, or if they were even permitted to breathe. Dr. Branch was proud of the example he had just made of the young man, and it was obvious by the thin smile that formed across his lips. He was in control, and in that one unexpected act of authority the recruits knew exactly what they had gotten themselves into. This man meant business, and if you were not careful, you'd be gone in seconds.

"I have no use for individuals like that at my company. He was so eager to please, that he failed to assess the situation before he acted. People who conduct business like that lose me millions of dollars, and I will not stand for it. Not even for a moment. In business, as in life, you must embrace the fact that you control every decision you make. You have a choice at every corner along the journey that is your existence, and if you take this challenge, this opportunity with me, you will learn and hopefully earn more than you ever dreamed possible."

Chapter 5

Cherise had been lying on her belly with her elbows on the porch and her innocent face cradled in her hands. She looked up at Richard and proclaimed, "That doctor man seems like a real butt-face."

Richard laughed at her perceptive remark and nodded in agreement.

"He is a butt-face, but if it weren't for Dr. Branch, I would have never met your great-grandfather."

She stood up, put her hands on her hips and said, "I guess, but I don't like him."

"You know what? I don't like him either, but I respect him."

"So you just snuck your way into the job?"

Richard thought for a moment and then said, "I suppose I did."

"Weren't you afraid you were gonna get caught?"

"Of course, but I had nothing to lose, so I just took a chance."

Cherise sat down next to Richard and asked, "What happened next?"

With a twinkle in his eye, Richard replied, "Should I keep going?"

"Yeah, keep going. When do you get to the part about my great-grandpa?"

"It's coming."

"Good, 'cuz I want to know everything about him."

Richard smiled and picked up from where he had left off.

Chapter 6

Dr. Alan Branch removed his dark blue blazer, draped it over the back of his executive chair, and sat down. His authority was absolute, and his intelligence was second to none. The young recruits were ready to learn all that Branch had to offer. As if they were all programmed with the same software, Richard noticed that everyone was sitting upright in their chairs, leaning forward, communicating nonverbal signs of attention, with pens at the ready.

Branch began slower this time—more targeted in his approach. These college recruits had been handpicked by his contracted headhunting agency so he knew just what they were and were not capable of achieving. Branch's expectations of his new team were clear. Lofty, but clear. They were going to help him grow X-Ray Query, LLC to a staggering $30 million of annual gross revenue in three years, which he knew from experience would earn him a buyout of at least $100 million when he put the company up for sale. After that, he had already formulated the plans for his next two business ventures: one in nanotechnology and the other in auto-cell regeneration, but for now, he stayed focused on the objectives of X-Ray Query, LLC.

"Let's start by opening the packet in front of you. Please understand that I know who you are, where you've come from, and just what you are capable of. That is why you are here. That is why you were handpicked from over 15,000 college graduates from around the world. You are my future leaders. You all possess the potential to do great things, so let's do the first great thing and fill out the employment forms on pages one, two, and three. Please be sure to sign and date all three pages and when you have completed this task, remove them from the packet and place them on the table in front of you."

Richard opened the X-Ray Query, LLC packet and began to read:

X-Ray Query, LLC (XRQ), a subsidiary of Branch International, Inc., is the next market leader in the x-ray imaging database catalogue and search retrieval market space. XRQ's flagship product, X-Ray Now, is an innovative and groundbreaking solution integrating software and hardware customized for the small, medium, and large medical health providers. XRQ owns sixteen patents and is the sole owner and controller of its technology. X-Ray Now provides an easy to master user interface with access to millions of digital x-ray images tied together through a seamless and secure world class network. Through a highly complex and proprietary state of the art query-based software application, the user can instantly retrieve digital x-

ray images based on user-defined search criteria.

The bio of the company went on for another few paragraphs, but Richard got the gist of it and was quite impressed with what the technology could do. He quickly realized how doctors around the world could pull up x-rays of their patients from any computer attached to the Internet. He understood the value of the information the imagery database could provide to patients and providers alike. A medical expert in China could instantly, and in real time, view the x-rays of a patient at a hospital in Nebraska and provide the primary physician with a second opinion. The medical world could collaborate as a seamless virtual community. Every question that popped into Richard's mind was answered in the company profile. Security and privacy issues were handled through digital image compression, file encryption, and proprietary expansion software. Millions of dollars had been poured into software development to ensure that during the compression and subsequent expansion, the integrity of the image would stay intact. A mis-diagnosis would not be caused by a reduction in image quality. The result was a pristine digital x-ray image, controlled by the patient and his doctor, which could be shared safely across the Internet and which would lead to improved patient care. Dr. Alan Branch was "The Man" and Richard knew it.

As fast as he could, he filled in his personal information and signed the first two pages. As he turned to page three, his eyes locked on a bold line midway down the page that read:

Annual Salary: $47,500 + Commission, Benefits, and Weekly Allowances

Before he could stop himself, Richard blurted out loud, "Holy Crap!"

As if the needle on an old record player just scratched across the LP, the entire room whipped their heads around to look for the verbal disturber. Richard joined in the look-around and acted as if he was also trying to identify the offender. He mouthed "Not me" to a few onlookers and dropped his eyes back to his packet in an attempt to right the rocking ship. The trainees abandoned their investigation and turned back to their respective paperwork. Richard pulled out Bruce's assignment sheet and started to scribble some numbers.

40 hours per week x 52 weeks per year = 2,080 hours per year
$47,500 divided by 2,080 = $22.84 per hour

Richard paused, took a slow, quiet breath, and exhaled nearly all the stress that had enveloped his body over the last few months. The only hurdle now was not getting caught. He had to fly under the radar, perform his job, whatever it was going to be, to the best of his ability and hope that Dr. Branch would not dismiss him as he had done to the poor kangaroo boy.

The last line on page three read:

If you accept the terms and conditions detailed in this contract, please sign and date below.

Richard put pen to paper for the third time and signed on for the ride of his life.

Chapter 7

Dr. Branch looked at the eager recruits and said, "I want to take a few minutes with you to set proper expectations. That way you will all have a better understanding of what you are getting into. I am a firm believer that experience is the best way to learn a new skill. You may have heard it described as 'drinking from the fire hose.' Well, that is precisely what you'll experience here. Over the next four weeks, I will provide you with the best training available on XRQ's technology. You will soon become experts on our products and services, but it will only be through live customer meetings that you will truly learn how to negotiate and close the sale. I can talk to you about principles of the Consultative and Strategic Sales Processes or Interest and Value Based Negotiations, but until you sit across the table from a customer and negotiate, all you'll have is information, not knowledge. Not know-how. With that in mind, do not expect me to teach you how to sell or to hold your hand during a negotiation. You'll need to figure that out on your own. I will give you the information, the tools, and the products to sell, and I expect you to sell them or we will unfortunately have to go our separate ways. Any questions so far?"

Collectively, the recruits shook their heads no, and Branch continued.

"If you would, please look around the room and take note of the determination in everyone's eyes. You all have high hopes and aspirations to succeed here, but despite those goals, my experience has shown me that 75 percent of you will not be employed here at XRQ in two months. Despite all of the research and investigation into your backgrounds and all of the training you'll receive, three-fourths of you will fall short. In order to help you prove me wrong, here are my rules that I expect you to follow, or you will most likely find yourself as one of the 75 percent.

"Number One: You will arrive at work, Monday through Friday, at 7:00 a.m. sharp, dressed like a professional, and you will not leave until you have completed every task you are assigned.

"By the way, young man in the back, are you trying to insult me with your casual attire today?"

Richard manufactured a bit of contrived confidence and spoke clearly.

"Of course not, sir. I mean no disrespect to you, your company, or my colleagues."

"It's 'Doctor,' not 'sir.' I have earned my title. Please make sure to use it."

"My apologies...Doctor. I mean no disrespect with my clothing."

Surprised, but pleased by Richard's articulate response and quiet confidence, Dr. Branch continued.

"I will presume your luggage was lost in transit, and it will never happen again?"

"It will never happen again, Doctor."

Richard stayed quiet after that, not wanting to continue telling lies about the old husband and wife dry cleaning team who accidentally triggered a lint fire in their shop that fully consumed his three wool and two tweed suits. None of it was true, and Richard thought it best to not pursue the imaginative excuse even if he was pressed further by the good doctor.

Branch was undecided if this orientation crasher had the skills to succeed at XRQ, but he knew it took guts to sneak into the office and pretend like he was one of the recruits. This underdressed novice was either a risk taker or a fool. Time would reveal which soon enough. Dr. Branch decided that he would play along with the charade to see what this kid had to offer. He continued.

"**Number Two:** You will spend no less than six hours every weekend preparing for the next week. If you do not, it will become obvious to me in your performance, and I will not hesitate to let you go.

"**Number Three:** You will make mistakes. I expect mistakes to happen. You are young and have not experienced every style of negotiation and until you do, it is only natural that you will make mistakes and stumble along your way. However, if you fail to learn from your mistakes, and the mistakes of the other trainees, I will let you go. I will attend every sales call with you until I determine that you are capable of representing XRQ on your own. If you make a mistake, I will let you know there and then in the room by simply taking control of the meeting, and you will sit quietly by and learn as I maneuver through the remainder of the meeting. I also expect that there will be times, after you make a mistake, when I will escort you out of the room if I feel that your error has put XRQ at a disadvantage. You will have until the next morning to give deep thought to your error. At 7:05 a.m. sharp, you will stand in front of the group and explain what you did wrong. If you articulate clearly what mistake you made and what you will do to correct yourself the next time, I will be glad to keep you as an employee. However, if you are unable to clearly express your understanding of your error, and the immediate action required to remediate, I won't hesitate to let you go. Any questions?"

Again, the room stayed silent as everyone shook their heads no.

"Seeing none, let us begin. Please pass your three signed pages forward."

Everyone carefully tore the pages along the perforation and passed them to the person seated in front of them. Dr. Branch was pleased with the group's obedience. After collecting all of the paperwork, he continued.

"Excellent. Let's start at the beginning. Please open your manuals and turn to the page that reads '*X-Ray Now*, The Future of Digital X-Ray Imaging.'"

In unison, the packets flew open, pens clicked to attention, and the recruits, along with the lone stowaway, were ready to set sail.

Chapter 8

The intensity of the first day left the twenty young professionals in a zombie-like state. Their eyes had glazed over, and no one could have prepared them for the guerilla training that had been forced upon them in the nine-and-a-half hours they sat in front of Dr. Alan Branch. Thirty minutes remained before the group would be dismissed for the day, and Richard struggled to stay alert. He felt his brain ooze like warm Jell-O from his ears. He thought about the slimy sensation and realized that with all the thinking he'd done that day, he had probably worked his brain so hard that he had melted his ear wax and it was not Jell-O at all, but actually his own inner ear waste trying to escape for its life. He was completely spent, but he was not alone. Each of the twenty future leaders had withered into lumps of soggy flesh with their ambition in puddles beneath their seats.

But Dr. Branch had not missed a beat. He had not stopped talking for even a moment. The man was a machine and would not fail in his quest to leave his mark on the world, or his short-term goal of identifying his "Top Five Recruits." The rest of the pack, the other fifteen, would not make it through the week. It was all part of his plan. Similar to the mental torture applied against prisoners of war, Branch needed to extract the weakness from his pool of resources and focus all his efforts on the lucky five.

"WAKE UP!!!! You all look like you have had enough, but the final topic of the day is the one, above all else, that you must fully understand. Your success or failure with this company may just be the result of how well you understand this concept. *The path from position to concession is a slippery slope.* Who can explain what that means and why it is so important to understand?"

This was a totally unexpected change of dynamics. Dr. Branch had been talking at the crowd for almost ten hours straight and now, when everyone in the room was completely spent, he expected an intelligent response. Ever so slowly, three hands rose like limp slabs of beef from the sides of their near dead carcasses.

Branch pointed toward a strapping lad who could have doubled for a young Clark Kent, had Clark been without his superpowers and had suffered the fate of a steamroller accident.

"You. Please stand, state your name, and share your thoughts with the room."

With that, the young man gripped the table in front of him and rocked his body to-and-fro, leveraging enough torque to propel himself to his feet. He rubbed the film from his eyes with a wipe of his hand and spoke in a careful and steady tone.

"Well, the idea that, oh, wait, excuse me. My name is Vincent Panelli. Well, my thought is this. How and where you position your products and services is very important. You have to position the sale at the right level or the customer will not be in a position to concede to the purchase, and if you fail to position your offer correctly you'll end up spinning your wheels trying to sell to people in positions that do not have the authority to buy."

Although Vincent's feet were wearily planted in the ground, he stood firm and hoped for some accolades from the boss. Dr. Branch, who had worn down the carpet in the front of the room during his day-long lecture, approached the fragile Superman. The room immediately filled with a concoction of one part excitement, two parts tension, and three parts nausea. For the first time in over four hours, everyone was focused and thinking the same thing at the same time. Did Vincent nail it, or was Branch going to stick a nail into Vincent's coffin? Dr. Branch stood a few inches away from Vincent. Just before speaking, he extended his left hand and pointed to the second of the three original risk takers.

"You. Please come here. Please stand next to Vincent and tell me your thoughts. Do you agree with Mr. Panelli's explanation?"

The young man, who stood a mere 5'3" tall, looked like a streetwise bulldog. He rose from his seat, steadied himself as he carefully walked around a few chairs to his mark on Vincent's left, and extended a recently sweaty, now freshly pants-dried hand to Dr. Branch.

"Doctor Branch, thank you for this opportunity."

Branch extended his hand at a forty-five degree angle down and pressed flesh with the pint-sized man. *"Decent start,"* Branch thought to himself as he allowed an inviting smile to encourage his employee.

"My name is Mark Kramer, and I am a recent graduate of the Wharton School of Business. I can say with confidence that Vincent missed the mark by a mile. I do not believe he understands your concept, and I feel that he grossly misrepresented the true meaning of the phrase, *The path from position to concession is a slippery slope."*

Branch paused for a moment, surprised by Mark's arrogance, and then replied:

"If that is so, and I don't know that to be true yet, what is your interpretation?"

With a little less confidence this time, Mark began again.

"Dr. Branch, I believe my interpretation is easy to explain, yet complex to apply. *The path from position to concession is a slippery slope* means if you have not properly prepared for your sales call, which includes many topics that you have covered today as well as others I'm sure you will discuss with us over the next few weeks, you weaken your ability to position your superior products and services to your customers. Once you are standing on unstable ground, you risk offering a series of financial, technical, and business concessions, or in layman's terms, customer giveaways, in order to avoid the loss of the sale. Therefore, you must prepare for all sales calls, stand firm in your position that you offer a quality product and do not simply concede your position of price, terms, and deliverables just to close the sale."

Mark took a deep breath, threw his shoulders back, and waited like a disciplined soldier. Branch backed up and sat on the table behind him. His legs were swinging back and forth just enough to suggest that something unexpected was about to happen. He was preparing to wield an iron fist, but out of the corner of his eye noticed that the young lady who had been one of the original three to raise her hand had all but allowed her chair to swallow her whole. She had sunk so low in her seat that her eyes were level with the desk. She was hiding in plain sight, and Dr. Branch shook his head in disappointment. The sooner he weeded out the weakness in the room, the faster he could dominate the market, recognize a profit and sell his business. His sole focus at this moment was to identify his top five employees. He called out to the young lady.

"Miss. Sit up please. I can see you hiding. You raised your hand and now it appears as if you've lost your arm and your desire to be here. I would like for you to contribute to this discussion. Would you please evaluate Vincent's and Mark's explanations of the concept of position to concession?"

The young lady barely sat up as she whispered her thoughts.

"I think Mark said it better."

Silence flooded the room. Everyone was waiting for the tidal wave that they knew was coming. They all thought Dr. Branch was gearing up to be the perfect storm and capsize the young woman and the kryptonite-laden Vincent. Branch jumped to his feet and returned to his position of power behind the podium. He laid his hands on both sides of the wooden lectern with the grace of a French mime and smiled.

"You, sir. In the back. Mr. 'I Lost My Luggage.' Please stand and have the final word."

Branch thought to himself, *"This kid's answer will determine his future here. If he wants to stay, he'd better answer wisely."*

A shot of anxiety ran down Richard's spine. He did not expect Branch to involve him in this trainee standoff. Richard peeled himself from his chair and stood. All eyes were glued to his every move, and he felt that now was the time to come clean and admit he had no right being there that day. He had been swept up in a wave of ambition that carried him up the elevator and into this conference room early that morning, but he was not one of the pre-selected few. He was not worthy of this opportunity. He was just a $12 per hour temp worker destined for mediocrity, but just before Richard opened his mouth, he froze. A crystal clear image of the convenience store hit him between the eyes. He saw himself as an overweight 40-year-old with male pattern baldness, bagging groceries for a group of arrogant teenagers as they pointed and laughed at what had become of his life. He gagged on the vision of his future and visibly shook the image from his head. If he was going to find success here, he would need to take risks. He would need to speak his mind. He would need to act with confidence and leadership. If he stayed silent, he knew he would seal his fate. So Richard spoke carefully and intelligently.

"Dr. Branch, I believe this is not simply an exercise to determine who understands the concept at hand. If you are asking me to pick between Vincent and Mark, I would have to agree with Mark's explanation. I could not have said it any better myself, but I don't believe that was your point here."

Intrigued, Dr. Branch leaned forward against the podium and said, "Go on."

"Based on your decision to dismiss the young man earlier, I view this as another test for us to pass in order for you to build the best sales team possible."

"Is that the case here? Is that what you think I am doing?"

"Yes, I believe it is."

"And if you are correct, then what do you recommend I do with the situation in front of me? If you were me, and be sure to think very carefully before responding to this question, if you were me and this was your business, your money, and your reputation on the line, what would you do?"

In his gut, Richard felt exactly as he had on every roller coaster he'd ever boarded. He was at that weightless moment at the very apex before the drop. It was the one moment you felt like you were floating in space. Your gut was in your throat and as long as you were not completely insane, you would hold on to the safety bar just enough to be sure you wouldn't be jettisoned from the cockpit. He knew what was coming next. It was the unavoidable plummet at mind altering speeds. No guts, no glory. Richard had boarded the ride of his life, so he took a breath and let it fly.

"Dr. Branch, if I were you and this was my business, I'd fire all three without hesitation."

Mark whipped his head around and shot eye daggers at Richard. Vincent, who twitched back and forth between Richard, Mark, and Dr. Branch, appeared to be looking for a mental escape route. The nameless girl sat frozen in her seat.

Chastising Richard like a father would speak to a disobedient toddler, Branch said, "Wow! That was a very bold statement. Explain yourself immediately."

Richard continued.

"It is my belief, Dr. Branch, that Vincent unfortunately was unsuccessful in his attempt to define the concept because he does not yet have the work experience to fully understand the nuances of negotiations. He appears to be a very nice man, and I would welcome a friendship with him, but as a representative of your company, and therefore someone who represents you, I do not believe he is what you are looking for. As for the young lady in front of me, she does not appear to possess the drive and confidence you require to move your company forward. Lastly, Mark. Although I believe his explanation was accurate, he expressed himself in a very rude manner. He insulted a stranger in front of you for your approval and his personal gain. I feel he acted disrespectfully, and I would prefer to not have someone like that on my team."

"What's your name?"

"Richard. Richard Cast."

With that, Richard shut his mouth and simply waited. And wait he did. No one said a word for quite some time. The silence lasted for a few minutes and all the while Dr. Branch was deep in thought as he carefully analyzed the dynamics among the four employees. Suddenly, Mark broke the silence with his attempt at a rebuttal.

"Dr. Branch, if I may, I do believe that..."

"Mark. Stop. Your comments will do you no good now. Richard is correct. You are an arrogant man, and you made the wrong decision today by speaking the way you did about Vincent. You should give plenty of thought to who you want to be, but you'll need to do that on your own. Thank you for investing your time with me today, and I wish you success wherever your career may take you. You may leave now."

Had this been high school, Mark would have already thrown Richard to the ground and pummeled him to oblivion, but now people get arrested for pulling stunts like that and Mark knew it. He pushed Vincent out of his way and like a bull in a china shop, knocked chairs and tables aside as he took the long route to the door so he could pass directly in front of Richard. Mark stopped inches away from Richard, and although his eyes were even with Richard's chest, they both knew Mark could do some serious damage. Richard strained to avoid eye contact while at the same time not reveal his fear. Richard won the silent standoff, and Mark left the room with a cloud of wrath trailing close behind.

With both arms, Branch pointed simultaneously at Vincent and the woman slouching in her chair.

"As for you two, thank you both as well for your time. Unfortunately, XRQ no longer requires your services. You may both leave."

And leave they did. Both Vincent and the woman who had never shared her name, bolted from the room without a word. It was only the first day, and Dr. Branch had already fired four people. The recruits that remained clearly understood that they were expendable. Being selected as one of the original twenty was a major accomplishment, but that would be nothing next to keeping their job. This CEO meant business, and if they were not at the top of their game every second of every minute, they would find themselves in a line heading out to the busy streets below. Dr. Branch looked at Richard, who still stood his ground in the back of the room, winked and said, "Richard Cast. Well done. Very well done."

Chapter 9

Cherise stood straight up, defiantly placed both fists on her tiny hips, and stomped her right foot against the floorboard. She was angry at Richard and shot him a look of disappointment that could only come from an innocent little girl. She thought she had been spending time with a kindhearted man, but now she had doubts.

"I told you that doctor man was a butt-face. I knew he was the whole time, but why'd you go and do that to those people? Why'd you have to go and be so mean?"

"Well, I had to, or I would have been thrown out as well."

"Yeah, but that don't make it right to be a butt-face like that."

Richard thought about it and said, "I guess you're right, but look at it this way. If I had not said what I said to Dr. Branch, I would have never met your great-grandfather and I wouldn't be here today. You would have never known what happened to him and that would be something you'd miss for your whole life."

Cherise let her arms fall to her side as she thought about Richard's comments. She knew right from wrong. She had been raised by a loving and compassionate family, so when she came face to face with unkind behavior, she called it as she saw it, but Cherise knew Richard was right. If he had given up and been fired that day or walked out on his own, she'd carry a hole in her heart for the rest of her life.

She softened her attack and said, "Don't go anywhere. I gotta go inside and tell my grandma that I'm outside here with you. When I get back, you better get to the part where you meet my great-grandpa or I'm gonna let you have it good. You got me, mister?"

Richard couldn't help but laugh. She was so adorable and had such a presence about her that she made him wonder, for the first time, about having children of his own.

"I'll wait right here for you, Cherise. I promise you'll hear about Chamberlain when you get back."

Cherise spun around toward the church door, and the evening air fluffed the ruffles in her dress. She skipped away and disappeared into the chapel.

Richard thought about where to pick up the story when Cherise returned. He knew she'd carry out her threat to let him have it good if his first words were anything other than, *"I met your great grandpa,"* but there was actually much to tell between that first day at XRQ and his first conversation with Chamberlain. His mind raced through the details of the two-week XRQ boot camp that depleted the once filled conference room down to the top five employees. Richard had somehow managed to outlast the best of the best from the University of Pennsylvania, U.C. Berkley, Princeton, and even one from Cambridge. He was proud of himself, but not nearly as surprised and proud as his parents. Despite all their threats, they truly wanted him to find his way into a successful career. For the time being though, the possibility of employment at the family store had faded like an old Polaroid at the bottom of a shoebox full of childhood pictures. It was faded, but it was still there. If Richard squandered this opportunity, he'd be holding that picture in front of his eyes for a very long time.

Dr. Branch crafted the training sessions to maximize everyone's time. Within two weeks, the five remaining sales reps had fully grasped the Technical and Operational Elements of the *X-Ray Now* application and infrastructure, just like Branch had promised on day one. Through role playing and debrief debates, everyone seemed to leverage the strength of the team to quickly grow the sales force into a powerful machine. They all felt confident in their ability to articulate the value of the *X-Ray Now* solution, but as Branch said on the first day, they would only master the art of negotiations through customer meetings. The fire hose drinking was just around the corner, and that would reveal who truly had what it took to succeed in Branch's world.

Cherise was taking longer to return than Richard had expected, so he rose from the steps and stretched his body as he made his way toward the back of the building. As he walked, he noticed the peeling paint, the missing wooden shingles, and the general tilt of the entire structure. It appeared that the church, much like a plant, had bent itself toward the sun, in order to receive the most nourishment this world could provide. Richard felt as tired as the church appeared, and he hoped that both would withstand another hundred years of existence. As he wandered the grounds, his mind drifted back to the morning of his first sales call.

Chapter 10

As the subway car came to a grinding halt at 6:45 a.m., Richard tried to grab hold of the metal pole to steady himself, but he missed and ended up banging his chest against it instead. The jolt popped the lid off his coffee cup, and a hefty gulp of his morning java spilled onto the floor. The subway doors opened, and he followed the herd onto the platform. With his lidless cup of coffee in hand, Richard could not stop imagining specks of subway gunk floating in the dark liquid, so he looked for a place to dump the coffee. Unfortunately, the trashcan by the stairs was being picked through by an elderly homeless man with a battered guitar strapped to his back, and as he contorted himself to get deeper inside, his left arm twisted around to hold the guitar close to his body. As Richard approached, he could hear the man mumbling to himself. It was mostly incoherent, but Richard swore he heard the homeless man say, *"I'm not a failure"* and *"It's not my fault, Mabel"* and *"Shut up, old man. Don't you tell me how to do my job."* Richard placed the cup of coffee on the floor beside the garbage can without disturbing the treasure hunt and then darted up the stairs, out to the city streets above, never once looking back to see if the coffee was discovered.

At 7:00 a.m., the five Client Executives, as they were now called, sat wide-eyed and attentive as Dr. Branch announced to the team that they were ready. The energy in the room was intense, and the three men and two women were beaming with pride. They were ready...they hoped. If Dr. Branch said it, then it must be true because there was no way he would put any of them in front of customers if he thought they could fail.

Branch opened a file as he stood behind the podium in the front of the room. He read it once more for his own satisfaction and then began.

"I want you to know that I am proud of you all. You have withstood a tremendous amount of abuse and manipulation over the past few weeks. However, you have all come out stronger for it. You are the best of the best, and I am confident that you will all achieve great things here at XRQ."

Richard, along with the other four, smiled and nodded as they allowed themselves a moment of self admiration.

"Unfortunately, now is when things really get tough. If you thought my training boot camp was grueling, you'd better strap yourselves in tight because, when it comes to customer meetings, you had best be at the top of your game or you may end up sitting next to me like a mime stuck inside his imaginary box. Remember, you are here to help grow this company quickly. When we are in front of the customer, I need you to treat each negotiation as if it were your company, your money, and your reputation on the line. I told you this many times before, but I will repeat myself one final time in order to ensure that you understand what I expect from you during your customer calls. Please understand that until you have built a client base, I will arrange and attend all meetings. Unless I tell you otherwise, I will initiate the conversation and then pass the meeting to you at the appropriate time. Your job is simple. Establish rapport with the customer, demonstrate that you are an expert in your field, and help them realize the benefits they'll enjoy by owning our solution. Do not offer a discount if you do not need to, but if the situation calls for it, you may give 10 percent off the list price for first-time-buyers. I have 30 percent more to play with, but that will be at my discretion. If you make a mistake along the way, and I expect you to make mistakes, I will take control of the meeting and you will sit quietly by my side and observe. Pay attention during these moments, for it is here that you will learn much about negotiations. However, if I determine that keeping you in the meeting after your mistake will jeopardize the sale, I may choose to walk you out of the room. Again, if I do allow you to stay, please do not try to interject your thoughts or ideas. Simply sit quietly for the remainder of the meeting and politely shake the customer's hand goodbye when they leave. Once the customer is gone, you will then immediately return to your home and prepare your presentation for 7:05 a.m. the following morning. In that presentation, I will expect you to explain what you did wrong and what you need to do next time. If you nail it, you stay and get to try again. If you don't, well, let's just say your new name will be Vincent."

After the quasi-motivational speech, Branch announced the five meetings scheduled for the day, and Richard was first on the list. He was instructed to meet Dr. Branch at 10:25 a.m. sharp in Branch's office, a room that had previously been off limits. They would be meeting with Doctors Miller and Goldblatt from a regional radiology lab who were looking to expand their offices in the Tri-State area. Richard was excited. He truly felt prepared to lead his first sales meeting. He had butterflies fluttering in his stomach, but knew that Dr. Branch had prepared him well for this moment.

The few short hours between the internal morning session and Richard's meeting passed slower than he hoped, so Richard kept himself busy by studying his manuals and running a series of role playing exercises in his head. 10:20 a.m. finally arrived, and he gathered his personal and business effects. He knew that he should arrive neither early nor late, but precisely at 10:25 a.m., so he headed to the restroom for one last bladder check and a quick personal grooming session. Richard stood in front of the bathroom mirror, looked himself deep in the eyes, and convinced himself that he was ready, and then headed out.

It was time for his career to begin. Richard sat quietly in Dr. Branch's office while Branch engaged in light conversation with the radiologists in the lobby. As the three men entered the office, Richard stood. He was nervous, but hid it well. As expected, Dr. Branch made the introductions.

"Dr. Miller. Dr. Goldblatt. I'd like to introduce you to Richard Cast."

Richard extended a hand to greet Miller and Goldblatt.

"Richard is one of my top Client Executives, and I have asked him to join us today to help you better understand how XRQ can help you accomplish your goals. Richard, why don't you take it from here."

This was it. The handoff had occurred. This was the moment of truth that Richard had been waiting for. He had to shine or he'd be bagging groceries next week. It was his first true sales pitch with real clients. No more role playing and debriefing with his peers. No more learning sessions and practice runs. His job was on the line, and he questioned his ability to succeed, but the thought of his career alternatives, or lack thereof, gave him the motivation to move forward. It was time to open wide and drink from the fire hose.

"It's a pleasure to meet you both today. Dr. Branch and I appreciate you taking time out of your day to give us this chance to talk with you about XRQ."

Goldblatt responded, "Thank you for having us."

Richard motioned to the chairs as he said, "Why don't you have a seat and I'll start by walking you through an overview of XRQ and the *X-Ray Now* solution."

Miller, Goldblatt, and Branch all sat while Richard made his way over to the large whiteboard against the far wall. Over the course of his training, Richard found it much easier to explain the elements and functionality of the solution by drawing a diagram that represented the medical facility, the x-ray machines, the XRQ hardware and software, a large cloud to show the Internet, and the user interface that would be accessed on the other side to retrieve the x-ray image. The first twenty minutes of the meeting were extremely encouraging. Richard's concise overview of the tools and technology rang true with the radiologists, and they both seemed to grasp the value that *X-Ray Now* could bring to their practice. They began asking the right questions that showed Branch and Richard their level of interest.

"So, what about security? How can we make our patients feel totally at ease that their private information will be safe?"

Richard responded with detailed information about XRQ's world class security features. He referenced the encryption software that was custom developed by a group of retired U.S. Marines who had previously worked on a covert engineering team focused on improving homeland security. The doctors were not only satisfied, but also impressed.

Then Dr. Goldblatt asked, "How will we be sure the images won't be fuzzy and unreadable after you compress and expand them? Your solution and the image itself will be useless to us if we can't read the x-rays."

Richard explained the technology behind the file size compression and expansion software and how XRQ had invested over ten million dollars in its development to guarantee image clarity. In fact, the legal contract explicitly guaranteed no degradation in image quality.

Again, the doctors seemed pleased with the response.

Then Miller asked, "So, how much does it cost?"

Richard knew the price question was going to be asked sooner or later, and he was proud of himself that he had prepared his exact response.

"Dr. Miller, the solution that I have shared with you today lists at $350,000."

Silence. Miller and Goldblatt were not expecting a price tag anywhere near $350,000. They were baffled and just sat there with stunned looks on their faces. Branch did not move. He waited to see what was going to happen and how Richard would respond. Richard held his ground by the whiteboard. He wanted to explain why the price was the price, but to his credit, Richard knew to keep his mouth shut. Then, without saying a word, the radiologists stood and turned toward the door. They were leaving. They had heard enough and had no intention of spending $350,000 today, tomorrow, or next year. Richard panicked. He knew that if he let Miller and Goldblatt walk out the door without trying to stop them, he might as well hand in his employee badge and follow them out of the building, so he spoke up.

"Just a moment please. I was not finished. I said the solution that I have shared with you today lists at $350,000. That is our list price. I know it is unexpected, but the improvements and expedited care you'll be able to bring to your current and future patients will quickly generate incremental revenue to offset the initial outlay of funds. Obviously, we would be glad to offer you a 10 percent discount as a first-time-buyer. Please sit back down so we can continue talking."

Miller and Goldblatt stood by the door for a moment and then, ever so slightly, smiled at each other. In unison, they turned back toward Richard and returned to their seats. Richard exhaled gently in order to hide his gratitude for their change of heart. His panic dissipated, and he felt his blood pressure ease, but despite the positive thoughts now swimming around in Richard's head, nothing could have prepared him for the humiliation and devastation when, out of nowhere, Dr. Branch placed a heavy hand on Richard's shoulder and walked him right out of the office. As Branch ushered Richard through the door, he mouthed the words, *"See you at 7:05 a.m."*

Branch pulled the door closed, and Richard stood alone in the lobby staring into space. *What happened? What had he done wrong?* He did exactly what Dr. Branch had told him to do. His brain spun like a top, and he had no clue what just took place or where to begin to figure out what he would be talking about the next morning. His career had ended before it even began and Richard felt like complete failure.

Chapter 11

"Mr. Richard.   Mr. Richard.   MR. RICHARD!"

Cherise came running around the back of the church, calling out for her storyteller. The flutter in her voice revealed her fear that Richard had disappeared, but when Cherise saw Richard in the overgrown grass behind the church, a huge smile swept across her face.

"I told you to stay on the steps. Why'd you wander off?"

"I just needed to stretch my legs. It's been a long day, Cherise."

"Well, my grandma says we're leaving in one hour so you gotta get telling and get to the part about my great-grandpa already. Please. You still haven't told me enough to change my mind about him."

"I'm sorry, Cherise. I'll get to it now."

As Richard continued his story, they slowly walked the perimeter of the church.

"My first customer meeting was a disaster. I really messed up, but I had no idea what I had done wrong and if I didn't figure it out by the next morning, Dr. Branch was going to fire me. After the meeting, I left the office without talking to anyone, and I headed for the subway across the street. I figured I would just go home and start thinking about the meeting. I replayed the conversation in my mind and tried to figure out on my own what happened, but I guess fate had a different plan for me."

"What do you mean?"

Richard looked down at Cherise, smiled, and said, "Well, here's what happened next."

Chapter 12

Richard descended the stairs of the subway at 8th Avenue and 34th Street as he had many times in the past few weeks. His plan was to board the E train and head home to prepare for his 7:05 a.m. review. As he pounded his way through the turnstile, he was visibly frustrated and carried a cloud of confusion around him. People took note and stepped aside. To make matters worse, an announcement scratched out over the P.A. system let the masses know the trains were running ninety minutes behind schedule due to a fatality on the tracks. As if the plug was pulled from a bathtub drain, as soon as the message ended, a flood of people appeared to be sucked from the platform as they ran above ground to look for alternate routes. Richard exhaled and let his head fall to his chest. He stood alone like a beaten man. At that moment, his life would change forever.

"Say now, son. Why so blue? It's just a train. There will be another one around the bend any time now."

Richard lifted his head and turned toward the back wall where he saw a frail old man sprawled out on the floor. He appeared to be in his late seventies and, by the filth and grime that had ruined his clothes, had obviously been homeless for many years. He had a patchy gray beard that visibly housed a potpourri of insects, leftover food, and general subway soot. His nearly bald head showed its age with weathered scabs and newly open sores. On his right foot was a black leather loafer with a paper thin sole and on his left was a once white, now brown sneaker with a hole prominently displaying his big toe. On his lap was a battered wooden guitar with only three strings, but he held it tight as if it were a child. Although his heart went out to people on the street, Richard had learned quickly in his short time in New York to avoid conversations with the homeless. His previous encounter had resulted in verbal abuse after he generously handed the man a one dollar bill. Apparently, a single didn't go as far as it used to, not even for the homeless. Richard manufactured a courteous smile and began to walk away, but the old man kept right on talking.

"Look here, son. There ain't no reason for you to fear me. I'm just trying to help you see the brighter side. Look at it this way. Once the next train comes, you'll get a great seat because everyone will be walking by then."

Richard realized the old man meant no harm and was just looking for some human connection. Come to think of it, Richard could use a little mental distraction from the Branch-induced anxiety, so he decided to take the bait.

"Thanks, sir. I appreciate the advice."

"Well, if it's advice you're looking for, you've come to the right place. I've got advice from my grandpop and my pop about life, women, and business. All you got to do is ask and maybe offer me something to eat."

Richard was intrigued. Was this just a crazy man looking for a handout? Something about this man was different from the average subway dweller. There was something about his voice that sounded truthful, fatherly. Richard reached into his briefcase and pulled a muffin out of a bag. He knew he had plenty of time to kill before the next train arrived, so he figured, for the cost of a muffin, this might be entertaining if nothing else. Richard tossed the muffin underhand toward the old man, and as it tumbled end over end through the air, everything seemed to slow down, as if the muffin were floating in slow motion. The old man cupped both hands and let the muffin fall into his palms.

"God bless you, son."

Richard shrugged and said, "Sure. It's nothing."

"No, son. It is very much something."

The old man held the blueberry muffin close to his nose and breathed the fresh aroma deep into his aged and smoke damaged lungs. He did not ravage the food as Richard had expected; instead, he took gentle mouse-sized bites, savoring each morsel. Then he pulled a fresh blueberry from the side of the muffin, popped it in his mouth, and smiled as it tumbled across his tongue. There was no doubt that it had been decades since he'd tasted a blueberry. A wave of brotherhood rushed over Richard, and he somehow felt at ease.

From the ground, he looked up at the young man and said, "How can I help you today? The only thing I can repay you with is my advice, so how can I be of service to you?"

"Seriously, sir?"

"Of course, son. I may be past my prime, but I once had a life and I'm quite sure that my life holds precious truths to the secrets of this world. By the way, my name is Chamberlain Zacharias Taylor III, but you can call me Chamberlain. May I ask your name?"

"Sure. It's Richard."

Chamberlain chuckled and said, "Now that's amusing."

"What's that?"

"Your name and my name, son. Richard and Chamberlain."

Richard did not follow, so he asked, "Why is that amusing?"

"Richard Chamberlain, the actor. Don't you know him, son?"

"I think I've heard of him."

"Well, he was one of the greats. So Richard, my guess is that you are not upset about the train and by the look of stress you're carrying, my guess is that you had a bad day at work. I know it ain't a woman thing, because no one has that bad of a fight with a woman before lunch time. So my money is on a bad day at work. Now you might not believe this, but many years ago, I was a successful businessman. I had my own company with hundreds of workers. So, in exchange for the delicious muffin, my payment to you is my business advice."

Richard was intrigued by the homeless man. Chamberlain had guessed right that Richard's frustration was about business. He wasn't sure though about the truth to Chamberlain's past. How could a successful businessman end up in a subway wearing clothes that had not been washed or changed in what appeared to be decades? But the train had not yet arrived, and he had no intention of walking home at this point. To Chamberlain's surprise, but more so to his own, Richard sat down on the subway floor right next to the old man and began to share the events that had unfolded earlier that day.

"You see, I was in this meeting with my new boss. I'm not going to go into what I do and what I earn or any of that stuff. Just know that my boss is a brilliant man who has succeeded more in the last ten years than I know I will in my life, and even though he's given me a chance to really become a part of something important, he's not a nice man. He is manipulative, condescending, and arrogant, and I'm totally intimidated by him. I was in a meeting today with a potential client, and I was doing a great job talking about our company and our solution. I've got the customers asking the right questions. They finally get to asking about the price, and I know that in all my training with my boss, he says we can give 10 percent off the list price for first-time buyers and that he can extend an additional 30 percent off for qualified customers. When I tell the clients that the solution costs $350,000, I see them both freeze. They were in shock and just sat there without saying anything. Then, they both got up and headed for the door. They were leaving. It was my first sales meeting, and it was about to fall apart. I asked them to stay and I threw out the 10 percent discount that my boss said I should use if the negotiation called for it. My boss got so angry at me that he actually pushed me out of his office. I don't know what happened."

Chamberlain erupted in a full belly laugh. He was hysterical. Richard jumped to his feet, preparing himself to defend his ground from this lunatic. He yelled directly at Chamberlain.

"What the hell are you laughing at, old man?"

Chamberlain tried to catch his breath and settle himself down. He was thoroughly entertained by the boy's inexperience and sheer buffoonery, but did his best to remain calm so he could continue this unexpected conversation.

"Sit down, you silly boy. Don't you see? It is so obvious why your boss threw you out of the room. Don't you understand what you did wrong?"

Richard finally let his shoulders drop, and along with it, his defiance to this unexpected authority.

"No, I don't know what I did wrong. That's the problem. He said we could give away 10 percent if we had to, so I gave it away, and he threw me out. Now I'm going to lose my job if I can't figure it out by tomorrow morning. I have to explain to my boss what I did wrong and what I should have done. If I can't do that, he's going to fire me."

"Sit your little rear back down and let old Chamberlain share some pearls of wisdom with you. Go on. Sit back down, son."

Richard plopped himself back down on the cold subway floor, hoping Chamberlain would deliver a miracle. He did not expect much though. He hoped for answers to his questions, but what he really thought was going to come out of the old man's mouth was a stray piece of the muffin. In truth, he still believed he was talking to a crazy man.

Chamberlain looked at Richard, and for the first time in over fifty years, he had a glimmer of hope in his eyes. Chamberlain did not regret his self-imposed sentence of poverty and shame. Out of love, respect, and honor for his father, as well as the respect for the families affected by his factory's downfall, he did what he had to do, but here before him was a young man in need. A chance for Chamberlain to make things right. A chance to pass on the wisdom his grandfather and father tried to teach him. A chance to one day be forgiven. Chamberlain extended his calloused hand with an open palm toward Richard.

"Richard, I am going to help you and by doing so, I will save your job, but you must be willing to make a pact with me when you shake my hand. I will help you today, tomorrow, and the day after that if you need, in exchange for two things that will be insignificant to you, but important to me. Are you willing to make this pact, Richard?"

Richard could not believe what he was doing, but without control over his mind and body, his heart lifted his hand toward Chamberlain. The two men pressed flesh in a binding pact. One hand as white as the young man's innocence and naivety and the other as dark as coal, turned black from the cruelty of time.

"Well done, Richard. You have taken the first step to your salvation. In exchange for my wisdom, you will promise to return and speak with me again. You will not forget that I have helped you and you will value me as a man, and hopefully one day, see me as a friend."

"Done. And the other?"

"When you return, please bring me something healthier to eat. Do you know how fattening that muffin was?"

The two men smiled at each other and a friendship was born. Chamberlain began his private negotiation lesson, and Richard's eyes and spirit lit up like a flame. He could not believe the wisdom and insight this old man had, and he savored every word just as Chamberlain had savored the fresh blueberry muffin. It became clear to Richard just what he had done wrong earlier that day in front of the radiologists. It was so obvious once Chamberlain explained it. Richard could not believe how foolish and sloppy his actions had been. Chamberlain was amazing, and Richard was in awe.

As the E train pulled away from the station, Richard stood at the window and watched Chamberlain shrink in the distance. He knew that by 7:05 a.m. the next morning he was going to be just fine, and so did Chamberlain. The entire ride home, Richard could not stop wondering how Chamberlain ended up on the subway floor.

As the train disappeared into the tunnel, Chamberlain smiled and said, "He's a good boy, Mabel. He's a good boy."

Chamberlain slammed his glass of whiskey on the kitchen table. The booze-coated ice flew through the air and shattered on the floor.

"Shut your damn mouth, Mabel. You don't know what you're talking about."

Mabel was crying and clutching their six-year old daughter Estelle in her arms. Chamberlain came home drunk nearly every day that year, but today was different. Today was not just any day. It was January 27, 1958, Estelle's birthday, and Chamberlain had lost everything. He had gambled on the horses and lost, so he drank. He had gambled on the ball games and lost, so he drank some more. He had gambled with the family business and lost, so he downed a bottle of booze and tried to make it all disappear, but there was no escaping his reality.

"You bastard! You destroyed everything your father and grandfather worked for. You think you know it all. You think your way is always the best way. Why couldn't you just run the business the way they taught you? Why'd you have to go and gamble with the factory? You're a damn fool!"

"You best watch your mouth, woman, or I've got half a mind..."

"That's right, Chamberlain. You do have half a mind and that's why you're in this mess."

Chamberlain leapt from his chair and tried to grab Mabel, but she sidestepped his drunken lunge. Chamberlain slipped on the melted ice and landed face-first on the floor. Blood trickled from his nose as he lay there moaning. Before he could turn over, two massive hands grabbed him by his shirt, yanked him up with brute force, and threw him back into his chair. When Chamberlain's eyes refocused, he saw Mabel's father, who was the foreman at the factory, staring down at him.

"How could you do this, boy? Why would you hurt the family like this? Your father and grandfather taught you well, Chamberlain. They taught you everything they knew, but you thought your way was better. You thought you knew better, didn't you? Didn't you, boy?"

"What do you know? You think it's all my fault, but you don't know nothing. I had no choice. You'll never understand. And what do you care anyway?"

"You best watch your mouth when you're talking to me, boy. You've destroyed my child's life with your foolishness. You're a disgrace to your family. Your father and grandfather were good men that I was proud to work for, and you destroyed everything they built. You were taught well by two of the best there ever was, and you drank it all away. You're a damn failure."

"I'm not a failure. I love my father. You'll never understand."

"Look at yourself, Chamberlain. You have no idea what you've done. Do you? You've destroyed us all. You've destroyed the whole town. There ain't no way these people are gonna survive now."

Mabel dropped to the floor and clutched Estelle deep in her arms. They were both crying and rocking back and forth.

"It's not my fault, Mabel. Estelle. Sweetheart. Please look at me. Poppa loves you, baby."

Mabel's father opened his palm, reached back, and smacked Chamberlain right across the face. He grabbed the drunken fool by the collar and threw him to the ground. Chamberlain curled up in a ball and looked up at the raging man.

"You killed everything we worked for. Fifty years of sweat and blood and love went into that factory. All you needed to do was do it the way you were taught, but you drank and gambled it all away. That's not what they taught you. You gave away everything to pay off your debts. You deceived us all, boy. You made deals with shysters when you should have been dealing with people the way your father taught you. I always knew my Mabel was too good for you. I always knew you was a loser."

"Shut up, old man. Don't you talk to me like that. Don't you tell me how to do my job."

"You're a damn fool, Chamberlain. You ain't got a job no more. None of us do."

The last thing Chamberlain saw was his father-in-law's boot coming toward his face. And   then,   darkness.

Chapter 13

At 7:05 a.m., Richard was alone in the hot seat at the front of the conference room. He assumed the other four Client Executives had successfully maneuvered unscathed through their first customer calls. Had he not met Chamberlain, Richard would have been sweating and fearing the worst, but instead, he sat confidently and calmly as he waited to share his newly found negotiation wisdom with Dr. Branch and his peers.

Branch was in rare form that morning as a result of the unexpected cancellation of his other four meetings from the day before. The potential customers all called moments prior to their meetings and canceled due to scheduling conflicts and changes of interest. So it would be poor Richard alone that would feel Branch's wrath that morning.

As Dr. Branch slammed the door open with a hostile thrust, he greeted the crowd with sheer venom.

"Cast. Stand up. Don't waste my time or you'll be on the street before 7:10."

Like a bottle-rocket launched on July 4th, Richard shot out of his seat and took center stage. He was relaxed, though, and Branch took note.

"Richard. Your error yesterday disappointed me. I expected more from you. Much more. After I dismissed you from the room, I turned the clients' perception around and convinced them to come back for a second meeting. After that, I informed the others in this room about your mistake. We are all eager to hear your explanation. It's time for you to save your job. You will have five minutes to demonstrate that you fully comprehend what you did wrong. You may begin."

Richard closed his eyes for a brief moment and an image of Chamberlain came into focus. He opened his eyes and spoke the words of wisdom that his new friend shared with him.

"I made a number of mistakes yesterday, but the most significant error can be summarized in one phrase. ***A negotiation is a marathon, not a sprint.*** And to be successful in negotiations, it's important to never be so eager to 'win the race' or 'close the sale' that you concede anything before its time."

Dr. Branch was visibly stunned. A wave of amazement swept over him, and his jaw dropped ever so slightly. Richard continued.

"After seeing the shock in the client's eyes when I told them the list price was $350,000, the fear of losing the sale took control of my better judgment and I stumbled. I reacted quickly without thinking things through. My first mistake was offering a discount simply to get them back to the table. I should have first asked additional questions to uncover the root of their concern about the price. Was it that they did not budget for a purchase that large? Perhaps we could finance the deal. Was it that they feared a slow Return-on-Investment? Perhaps I could have shared market data on revenue potential that would have eased their concerns. Was it that they did not fully understand all of the attributes and benefits of the product that we believe justify the price? Perhaps I could have offered to walk them through a live demonstration, but instead, I offered a measly 10 percent first-time buyer discount hoping to stop them from walking out the door. I succeeded in keeping them in the room, which I'm proud of, but the manner in which I accomplished that was completely wrong. In one of our training sessions you told us that we could offer 10 percent off the list price if the negotiation called for it, but you never said that we had to offer the full 10 percent all up-front. The fact that I gave away everything I had control over was foolish, but offering the full 10 percent all at once was frankly stupid. It also indicated that I had additional room to move on my price. When offering a discount, if a round number like 5 percent or 10 percent is used as a first giveaway, that could indicate there are additional increments of similar percentages available for upcoming concessions.

In the future, when a pricing concession is required, I will never offer a round figure as a discount simply to move the negotiation forward, but instead, I will base all financial concessions strictly on the financial merits of the deal, whatever the percentage works out to be, 6.37 percent, 12.11 percent as examples. Also, I realized that my initial understanding of the first-time buyer discount was backward. I thought the 10 percent discount was there to get the customer's foot in the door and then they'd receive less than 10 percent on future purchases. I thought the 10 percent off was exclusive to the first purchase only, but now I realize I was wrong. It is not unreasonable to think that a customer's second, third, or fourth purchase would have a discount of 15 percent, 20 percent, or even 25 percent off the list price. By offering the 10 percent to the radiologists yesterday, I set a discounting threshold that would need to increase in the future. Had I offered 3.64 percent or 4.77 percent instead of the full 10 percent, we would have the potential to sell additional systems to them for more money down the road. I realize now how foolish it was to offer the 10 percent discount just to get them back to the table. This mistake will not happen again. In summary, never be so eager to close the sale that you concede anything before its time because *a negotiation is a marathon, not a sprint.*"

Richard checked the clock on the wall and it was just turning 7:10. He had spoken for five minutes straight and explained the root of all his mistakes just as Chamberlain had told him to. He panned the room, and the other Client Executives looked dumbfounded. They never expected Richard to deliver such a concise and insightful explanation. Richard wished Chamberlain could have seen him in action.   Chamberlain would have been proud of his new pupil.

Dr. Branch rose from his seat.   His entire demeanor had changed from when he had burst into the room minutes before.   He had been a tiger locked in a cage, but now moved slowly to the conference room door. His expression was one of bewilderment. *Who was this kid?*   Branch had never met anyone who was able to turn things around in one day as Richard had.   *If he knew so much, why did the mistake happen in the first place?*   As he stood by the door, he turned toward Richard and said three simple words.

"Well done, Cast."

As the door closed behind him, Dr. Branch headed straight for his office to call Doctors Miller and Goldblatt.   It was time to schedule the follow-up meeting.   This time he thought Richard would surely blow them away. *That kid has something that the others don't.* He knew it the moment Richard took control the first day and fired Vincent, Mark, and the shy young woman.   Dr. Branch sat down behind his desk and called the radiologists.

The receptionist answered and said, "Offices of Doctors Miller and Goldblatt, how may I help you?"

"Dr. Miller, please."

Chapter 14

With a bottle of water, an orange and a massive turkey club on rye with mayo, mustard, and coleslaw dripping from the side, Richard sprinted from the corner deli down to the subway platform. He could not wait to tell Chamberlain what happened and to thank him for his advice. Chamberlain was telling the truth all along. He really did know how to negotiate. Richard could not wait to hold up his end of the pact. Not just to deliver a healthy meal, but to really talk with Chamberlain in hopes of finding out more about negotiations and Chamberlain himself.

Richard pushed his way through the turnstile and jogged over to where Chamberlain was seated the day before, but the floor was empty, as if the old man never existed. Richard was confused. In his mind, Chamberlain did not appear to have enough strength to stand up, let alone walk away. *Why was he not here? Where could he have gone? How would he find Chamberlain to thank him and feed him and talk to him?*

Richard waited on the platform and counted eight trains as they passed by before he decided Chamberlain was not coming back. He took a pen out of his jacket pocket, wrote a note on the outside of the white paper deli bag and placed the food on the floor right where the two men had shared a moment in time. The note simply read:

Chamberlain,
I brought you something a little healthier to eat.
I hope you get the chance to enjoy it.
I look forward to seeing you again soon.
Your friend,
Richard,
PS- You were right. Thank you!

****

ANALYSIS OF PRINCIPLE #1

A negotiation is a marathon, not a sprint.

It is critical that a negotiator remembers to never be so eager to close the sale that he concedes anything before its time. I believe that this is one of the most basic tenets that every negotiator should understand; however, just knowing the principle is meaningless if you don't follow it, and that is why it is presented here. All too often, we understand the principles intellectually, but we fail to put the skills into practice when we're in the midst of the give-and-take. Although many negotiators know this principle and follow it, even seasoned negotiators make the mistake of conceding something too soon when the finish line is not coming fast enough or when the finish line is just in sight. Although it was Richard's inexperience that caused him to stumble and throw out an unwarranted 10 percent discount to the doctors just to get them back to the table, generally negotiators give things away before they need to because they are impatient, uneducated, unprepared, or simply being clumsy.

So how do you learn when the time is right to concede something? What is the rule here? How do you ensure that when you give something away, such as the 10 percent discount, that it's not too soon and that the concession does not compromise your position in the negotiation? The answer is simple. It depends. It depends upon what is at stake. It depends upon the variables of the negotiation. Unfortunately, the right time to concede is never the same because no two negotiations are the same. The only way to learn how and when to properly offer a concession is to experience it in a real negotiation and feel it in your gut. When you are actively negotiating with important factors at stake, with practice your emotions will tell you if you've offered a concession too soon. We can understand the concepts intellectually and we can follow a pre-scripted plan of give-and-take, but the only way to capture the information in your head and make it knowledge that translates into effective action during a negotiation is to experience the highs and lows of a real negotiation. It's understandable if you make a few mistakes along the way, but like Richard and his peers, you must learn from those mishaps and use your newfound knowledge to improve your negotiation skills.

This brings us back to my comments in the introduction where I talked about the human element of negotiations. In Chapter 7 Dr. Branch says, "I can talk to you about principles of the Consultative and Strategic Sales Processes or Interest and Value Based Negotiations, but until you sit across the table from a customer and negotiate, all you'll have is information, not knowledge." The way I like to explain this concept is by comparing information to a ball of wax sitting on the top of your head. You know it's there. You understand the concept, but it's all academic, and a negotiation is anything but academic. It is only when you are in the heat of the negotiation that the ball of wax that contains the information melts and runs down your body that you'll fully understand its meaning. When the wax has melted and you feel its warmth on your face and neck and shoulders and back and arms and in your gut, that's when you transform information into knowledge. Knowledge is acquired through experience, not through reading a concept in a book. So get out there and negotiate. Branch questions Richard's abilities in Chapter 13 when he thinks to himself, "*If he knew so much, why did the mistake happen in the first place?*" Understanding the information and knowing how to use it effectively is what separates the novice from the expert. And that principle applies to everything in life, not just negotiations.

I would be doing you a disservice if I did not at least share the framework around how, when, and why I offer my first concession. But again, no two negotiations are the same, so please accept these concepts as guidelines to maneuver within and not rules set in stone that must be followed in a specific order. To begin, I do not support the belief that the one who concedes first loses. I often make the first concession as a gesture of good will and to demonstrate that I am ready to enter into faithful negotiations with the hope of reaching a mutually beneficial agreement. I don't always concede first, but I never enter into a negotiation with the mentality that I will only offer my concession after the other party offers theirs. Anyone who locks themselves in like that limits the potential outcome of the negotiation.

So how do I make a concession that does not compromise my position? Two words: ask questions. You should ask questions until there are no more questions to ask. And once you've asked all the questions you can think of, come up with a few more and keep asking. "Doctor Miller, what do you think your patients would say about *X-Ray Now*?" "How has technology impacted your medical practice in the past five years?" "What are your competitors doing to attract new patients?" "Of the medical advancements you have adopted over the past few years, which have had the most and the least effect on your business?" "How would you see *X-Ray Now* fitting into your plans for expansion?" "Can you share any concerns you may have with the product and services?" "Do you see any areas of your business that *X-Ray Now* would negatively impact?" "If you do not move forward with this purchase, how would that positively or negatively impact your business?" "If you did purchase our solution, what would you expect from our company in order to ensure you get the most out of the technology?" I could go on for hours, and that's exactly what Richard should have done when the doctors began to leave the room after he told them the price was $350,000. A series of well thought out questions will reveal the buyers' wants, needs, and desires that ultimately influence the purchasing decision. The more you seek to understand the truth behind the buyers' decision, the faster you'll create a mutually beneficial agreement.

Once you've exhausted the questions and the other party has provided all the information they are comfortable sharing at that time, someone needs to move the negotiation forward by offering something. If nothing is offered, the negotiation stalls, and both parties could potentially lose. If I were Richard and I had asked all the juicy questions above and learned all I could, my next question would be the one where I ask for the sale. "Doctors Miller and Goldblatt, now that we agree *X-Ray Now* can improve the quality of the care you provide to your patients, will help you achieve your business objectives, and has a healthy return on investment, are you ready to move forward with the agreement?" If they still said no because the price was truly beyond their budget, the next thing I would need to do, if I was not going to return to questioning and establishing more value in my solution, is to decide if it is time for me to offer a concession. When it feels right to be the first to offer a concession, I have found success throughout my career by **testing a potential concession** or **extending a conditional concession** instead of flat-out offering one. Testing a potential concession with a buyer might sound like this: "If I consider being flexible with my asking price, how might that influence your decision to move forward with the agreement?" This potential concession test is carefully worded. I have not offered anything concrete nor locked the other party into a commitment, but it tests the waters to see how ready they are to buy. It also shows them that if they're willing to exchange their money for my goods, I'll be right there to help make their buying decision a little easier.

A different way to gain insight into the other party's eagerness to buy before truly offering a concession of value is by **extending a conditional concession**. A conditional concession sounds similar to the potential concession test but has a little more meat to it. The conditional concession sounds like this: "If I were to move a little off my asking price, would you be ready to sign an agreement today?" Here we've moved from concept to action. Whereas the potential concession test is more about intentions, the conditional concession is about their commitment to take action. It is a yes-no question. If I discount, will you buy? Instead of, if I consider offering a discount, would that influence your decision to buy? The two concepts are similar, but have different purposes. With that said, they are both powerful techniques to help you determine if you should or should not offer a concession. If the other party responds to your potential concession test or conditional concession with a yes, it is safe to assume that they are ready to begin actively negotiating the deal. If they say no, the first thing you should do is ask them why so you can begin to uncover additional reasons for their hesitation. Again, the more information you can gather, the better your chances will be in creating something special for both parties.

At this point, if Richard followed the suggestions above, he would have a solid understanding of the doctors' needs versus their wants, he would have established the value of his company and the solution, and he would have built a respectful business rapport with the doctors. If Miller and Goldblatt were still not ready to sign an agreement and Richard felt he would not compromise his position in the negotiation by offering a discount based upon the financial merits of the deal, this might be an appropriate time to extend his first concession. It's too early in the negotiation to consider a small discount a bad deal for X-Ray Query, LLC, and by offering something in an act of good faith, the stalled negotiation moves forward. One important point with offering any concession is being sure to get something in return. A negotiation is a series of two sides giving and taking. If one party offers a concession, it's critical to get something in return in order to ensure both sides are working toward a mutually beneficial agreement. Even if that "something in return" is just the other party's acknowledgement that you've made a gesture to move the negotiation forward, that give-and-take is the foundation of building lasting relationships.

As mentioned above, there is no rule that works for every negotiation, and some of you reading this might have taken a different approach. That is to be expected, and it proves the original point that when you negotiate with living, breathing human beings with their own opinions, ideas, and feelings, no two negotiations will ever be the same. Every give-and-take is unique, but if Richard offered a small discount here and I was Dr. Branch, I would support Richard's decision. But remember: never be so eager to close the sale that you concede anything before its time because ***a negotiation is a marathon, not a sprint.***
****

Chapter 15

"Richard, I was impressed with your analysis this morning. You articulated the primary concession error correctly, and your understanding of the secondary issues that you created by making the first mistake was right on target. Good job."

Richard was surprised by Dr. Branch's comments. It was the first time he'd seen Branch let his guard down and reveal a bit of compassion. It was also the first time that Richard felt truly guilty about deceiving his boss and his teammates. Although what he said earlier that morning was accurate, the words were not his own. Richard was merely the relay man sharing someone else's wisdom, but for now, Richard would take credit for Chamberlain's commentary and try to use it to advance his career. As the two men sat in Dr. Branch's office waiting for the arrival of the radiologist team's return visit, Dr. Branch set the agenda.

"Richard, I'd like for you to take the lead this time when Doctors Miller and Goldblatt arrive. Do not mention the previous error or the fact that you were disciplined for the mistake. Appear in control. You have been well trained, so have confidence in yourself. Never forget what I taught you about successful negotiations. In order to have a successful negotiation, at a minimum, there are three elements that must never change. First, you must ensure that both parties' interests are met. Not simply the stated wants and desires, but the underlying interests that motivate individuals to act. You must always look for the win-win in the deal or you should not accept their money. If both parties in the negotiation are not satisfied at the end, there will be no future business, guaranteed. Second, clearly demonstrate that you are an expert in your field. If you show customers that you know your products and services and your competitors' products and services better than anyone else, they will look to you as a trusted advisor, and trust is a critical element in every negotiation. Third, never forget that we are dealing with human beings with feelings. You must establish a rapport with them and be sure to never lie, cheat or deceive your customer. Act with integrity at all times, or you will fail in business and in life."

After the "How to Negotiate" mini-review, Dr. Branch updated Richard on the outcome of the meeting after his dismissal yesterday. Other than the 10 percent discount that Richard had mistakenly given away, no other concessions had been offered. Dr. Branch had effectively justified the cost and value of the product, and the good doctors were very much interested in learning more.

Richard and Dr. Branch agreed that a successful first sale to a well respected practice like Miller and Goldblatt's would quickly confirm XRQ's value in the marketplace and ultimately lead to a national presence in the targeted time frame. The strategy with Miller and Goldblatt was simple. Once Richard had completed his formal demonstration of the solution, the discussion would focus on helping the doctors see that, with the *X-Ray Now* technology in place, they could more efficiently and effectively operate and grow their practice without ever sacrificing the quality of care that their patients had come to expect and demand. In fact, with *X-Ray Now*, the quality of patient care would dramatically improve. Once past that discussion, Richard would make his first pass at closing the sale. He was to offer no additional price concessions since Branch had already moved past the pricing objection. If he encountered any additional pushback, he was given permission to offer flexible payment options and a few elegant negotiables like onsite training, an annual system maintenance check, and limited telephone support as incentives to help come to an agreement.

As soon as Richard and Dr. Branch finished discussing their position and strategy, Branch opened his office door and offered a welcoming smile and a wave to Miller and Goldblatt who were seated comfortably in the plush leather chairs in the lobby. Branch ushered them into the office and then took a seat behind his desk. It was now time for the second episode of *The Richard Show* to begin. Hopefully, he would not flop as fast as so many of the yearly television pilots do. Richard took a deep breath and began his career again.

"Gentlemen, it is a pleasure to have you back with us today to explore the innovative technology of the *X-Ray Now* application. As you know from your previous discussions with Dr. Branch, our solution enables healthcare providers from all fields to access digital x-ray images from a local and global database for the purpose of creating a Faster Time to Diagnosis and Faster Time to Cure, what we simply call FTD-FTC. I'm sure you can imagine the benefits of real-time high resolution digital image file sharing with experts around the world. Seamless local and global healthcare collaboration is the future of personalized patient care. The future is here, gentlemen, and there is no turning back."

Richard had started brilliantly. Miller and Goldblatt were close to salivating over the potential this technology would bring to their front door. When it came time to walk to the lab for a hands-on demonstration, Goldblatt knocked his partner to the side in order to be the first one out the door.

The demonstration was extremely effective. The massive bandwidth that the fiber optic cables provided instantly carried crystal clear images from the server to the work station. Miller surfed through x-rays of Canadian bone cancer patients from the 1940s and then, with a mere click of the mouse, jumped ahead sixty years to view the x-ray of a Jamaican man with lymphoma. The most impressive part of the demonstration was when Richard sat at the sister console next to Miller and launched a virtual Internet meeting where both monitors were able to view the same x-ray image at the same time. Richard lifted a plastic pen-like tool from the holster mounted on the side of the monitor. Until this moment, Miller and Goldblatt had not realized that the monitors were touch-screen enabled. Richard used the pen to draw circles around fractures and added notes like "Ouch" and "Crack!" on top of the image. While Richard was drawing on his screen, the x-ray image on Miller and Goldblatt's screen immediately updated with Richard's markings. Miller made the analogy to John Madden's on-screen drawings during a Monday Night Football game. Richard holstered the pen and turned the systems off. He looked at the radiologists, smiled and said, "Well? Should I wrap one up for you?"

Miller had the checkbook out and was just about to put pen to paper when Goldblatt asked for a caucus so the two men could talk. The break was honored, and the four agreed to meet back at Dr. Branch's office in ten minutes.

Despite the fact that Richard and Dr. Branch were alone in Branch's office now, the two men sat in silence. Richard attempted to discuss the sale with Branch, but was cut short when the door opened. Miller and Goldblatt entered the room and appeared to be ready to negotiate. They took their seats. Miller leaned back and crossed his legs while Goldblatt pulled his chair right up to Branch's desk, set his elbow on the mahogany top, and started to speak.

"Dr. Miller and I agree that your technology is amazing. We understand the benefits it will bring to our practice, and it is obvious that your product will enhance the healthcare industry. Overall, we are extremely impressed, but truthfully, we have a major concern."

Richard expected this type of discussion and did as he had been trained to do. He sat silent and let the customer do the talking. Richard knew he should sit quietly and let Dr. Goldblatt share his true thoughts and feelings. Two ears and one mouth on every salesman means listen twice as much as you speak. So Richard did just that and allowed his body language to express the message of *"Please, continue."* Branch, like a great teacher, was modeling the same behavior. Goldblatt began again.

"We performed a tremendous amount of research on you, Dr. Branch. You have quite an impressive track record. Your success is a direct result of your commitment and intelligence. Your technology, although young, is stable and we feel it will have longevity in this business, but we are people-people, Dr. Branch. We work in the people business. We deal with the realities of life and death of real people, not machines. Dr. Miller and I have grown successful in business and in our personal lives by surrounding ourselves with people we trust, people we admire, and people we respect. With that said, our concern with moving forward here today has nothing to do with your product. Our hesitation is about you, Dr. Branch. If we move forward with you, not just with your company and your technology, but with you, Dr. Branch, can we trust that you will be here to support us long-term? Can you convince me that you have the same objectives as we do—to help people? I bring this up because, although we admire you, we are uneasy with what appears to motivate you. We cannot put our patients at risk today, tomorrow, or ten years from now by entering into an agreement with people who might have different goals."

With that, Dr. Goldblatt slid his chair away from Branch's desk and sat quietly. He was trying to persuade Dr. Branch to not sell the business to the highest bidder. Miller sat by and struggled to maintain eye contact with Richard or Branch. It was evident now who was the senior partner at their practice. Richard held his breath and looked to Branch for a response, but he was met with a blank stare. Branch, although vulnerable at this moment, was as steady as a rock, or at least that's how Branch appeared to Richard. *Why was he not responding to Dr. Goldblatt's direct question? Why was he just sitting there?* After a pregnant pause, it dawned on Richard that it was his show. He was in control, and Dr. Branch's expectations were for Richard to respond and lead the discussion through to the end while Branch sat back and watched his pupil grow. Richard's Adam's apple popped up into his throat, and a vision of big Bruce from the temp agency came to mind. He knew that if he failed here, he'd be back at Bruce's desk with his tail between his legs, begging for another $12 per hour job. So he forced the lump from his throat with a targeted gulp and addressed the doctors seated in front of him.

"Dr. Goldblatt, I first want to thank you and Dr. Miller for investing your time with us. I appreciate that your time has a price, and I will not waste a second of it here by delaying our conversation in any way. The fact that you see the potential with our technology is fantastic. You are men of vision and I respect you for that. Since the only roadblock before us today is your concern with our long-term plans as a company, I would like to share our vision with you. You are right in your assessment of Dr. Branch. He is a brilliant man. He understands that beyond the hardware and software, we are in the people business as well. This company, its core values and leadership are here for the long run. Every year, new advancements will be discovered, and we will nimbly adjust to the changing dynamics and relationship between technology and medicine. Dr. Branch will steer this ship throughout its journey and guide its employees and customers like you, for many years to come."

With that, Dr. Branch stood, stepped around his desk, pushed a piece of paper into Richard's hand, and walked Richard out of the office, again. As Richard stood alone in the lobby, he unfolded the paper. He knew exactly what it was going to say.

See you at 7:05 a.m. tomorrow

Dr. Branch disappeared back into his office to save the sale. Richard's mind was spinning. He had made his second critical mistake and had absolutely no idea what he had done. His heart was pounding and he felt like he was going to be sick. He grabbed his head with both hands and fell back into the leather chair. *What happened?* Everything was going fine, but something went terribly wrong.

As he sat like a lump of melting fudge on a hot summer's day, one name came to mind—Chamberlain.

Chapter 16

Richard bolted from the office and headed straight for the stairs instead of waiting for the elevator. By the time he reached the stairwell of the fourth floor, he was out of breath, so he slowed his descent for the remaining floors which gave him time to gather his thoughts before he exited onto the ground floor. He pushed his way through the revolving glass door and joined the hustle and bustle of the New York City streets. Keeping true to his pact, he detoured to the corner deli once more and ordered a burger and fries for himself and chicken salad with low-fat ranch for Chamberlain. He grabbed two bottles of water from the case, swiped his debit card, and took off for the subway.

Richard wondered if Chamberlain would even be there today. He thought about the possibility of finding a vacant platform and how that would seriously damage his chances of solving the mystery behind his second mistake. Chamberlain had to be there this time. Richard needed Chamberlain's help, and if he was not in the subway station, Richard knew his fate would be sealed.

He lifted the bag of food over the whipping metal flow control bars, squeezed through the turnstile, and popped out on the other side. The station was packed with people of all sizes, colors, and ethnicities. It was a microcosm of the world above with the potent difference being the smell. Down below reeked of whiskey-scented urine, while up above, the stench favored rotting garbage.

Richard pushed his shoulders against the sea of transients and muscled his way to an open area towards the back wall. As he regained his footing, his eyes grew wide with hope. Chamberlain was back at his post, this time sound asleep with his head weighing down on his chest and both arms flopped over his battered guitar. Even in his sleep, Chamberlain held that guitar close to his heart as if guarding it from the outside world. Although Richard had spent less than one hour with the old man, he assumed it had been years since Chamberlain actually strummed the remaining strings of the splintered instrument. It had become more of a companion than anything else. Richard admired the frail man from afar. Although Chamberlain looked like someone's old laundry thrown out to rot, Richard did not fear that he had died. Instead, he laughed at how loud Chamberlain was snoring. Richard eased himself down to a comfortable position on the floor next to his friend.

Nearly an hour passed as Richard waited for Chamberlain to open his eyes. His burger and fries were long gone when Chamberlain snorted and let out a growl as he came back to life. As Chamberlain picked his head up, his eyes came to focus first upon the chicken salad and then just beyond, on Richard himself. Chamberlain was just as happy to see the food as he was to see his friend, but casting manners aside, he grabbed the salad and began shoveling fistfuls of lettuce, tomatoes, croutons, and grilled chicken down his throat. He ripped open the pouch of dressing and sucked its contents dry. Richard pushed the water into Chamberlain's hand and watched as the old man guzzled the entire bottle in one extended gulp. Less than two minutes had elapsed and Chamberlain had devoured the food, the water, and in his haste, a portion of a napkin and a piece of foil that once held the fat-free ranch.

"Richard!"

"Chamberlain!"

"So good to see you again, my son."

Richard smiled and said, "Good to see you too, Chamberlain. Did you get the turkey sandwich I left for you?"

"No, I did not."

"Well, I left you a turkey sandwich here, but I figured someone else would take it before you got back."

Chamberlain shrugged his shoulders and said, "Leftover food has legs around here."

"I assumed as much. Guess what?"

"You tell me, son."

"Well, Chamberlain, the advice you gave me about negotiations being a marathon, not a sprint was right on target. I said it exactly like you told me to, and my boss was blown away."

"Congratulations. You kept your job, and you kept up your end of our pact and brought me something good to eat. That must mean only one thing. You need more advice from old Chamberlain."

With his head held low, Richard replied, "Yes, I do."

Chamberlain put his hand on Richard's shoulder and said, "Why don't you start at the beginning and tell me everything."

Chapter 17

Chamberlain listened as Richard retold the events that had unfolded earlier that day. Occasionally, Chamberlain said, *"Oh"* or *"I see"* and even *"You don't say,"* but for the most part, he listened and waited patiently. Richard finished his story and then asked, "Can you help? Do you know what I did wrong? I really need your help here."

Chamberlain rustled Richard's hair with his calloused hand and looked him in the eye.

"Boy, that was one stupid mistake. That boss of yours was right to throw you out. Let me shed some light. You see, son, what that Dr. Goldblatt did was one of the oldest negotiation tricks in the book."

Richard sat quietly as Chamberlain began to speak. Once again, the old man had seen right through the fog and cut to the core of the issue. Chamberlain carefully phrased his thoughts and wisdom in a way that made Richard feel like he was in the presence of a prophet. Despite his successful years at Ohio State and his accomplishments during Branch's version of boot camp, Richard never once understood the art of negotiation like he did that day as he sat beside the withering sage.

When Chamberlain finished bringing things into focus for Richard, he said, "Son, I'm a bit tired now. I think I'll rest a spell."

And before Richard could promise to return with more food or even say thank you, Chamberlain's head hit his chest and the snoring echoed throughout the subway once again. Richard gathered his belongings and boarded the next train back to his apartment. Come 7:05 a.m. the next day, he'd be ready.

Chapter 18

The next morning as Richard entered the conference room, he expected to see the other four Client Executives sitting in the back of the room, while an empty front row beckoned his name, but to his surprise, two of his peers were seated at the head of the class. He assumed they must have stumbled as badly as he had to end up as one of today's Three Stooges. At exactly 7:05 a.m. Branch pushed his way through the door to find more than half his sales force in their respective dunce chairs. The only things missing were the white cone hats and a long wooden ruler to beat them with, but Branch would let his words take the place of the whipping stick. One at a time, Branch called each disappointment up to the front of the room and instructed them to share their analysis of their mistake. The only thought running through Branch's mind was how much time it was going to take him to recruit and train a second round of college graduates. This crop had been a major disappointment.

The first to address the group was one of the women. She skated by with a copycat rendition of Richard's lesson from the day before. A little less eloquent and a lot less convincing, but she still fundamentally understood to not discount before she was asked. Satisfied, but not impressed, Branch made her sit in the back of the room by herself so she could think about what she did wrong.

The only other less humiliating thing than losing her job would have been if there was a chalkboard in the room for her to scribble, *"I will not discount before I'm asked"* one hundred times. Instead, she sat down as instructed and distanced herself from the next speaker and the two-time offender. For now, she was one of the lucky ones that got to keep her job.

The next to present was one of the other men on the team. He took center stage and failed miserably. He racked his brain all night, and when he got to the front of the room, all he could do was apologize for not being able to figure out what he did wrong. He did not explain what mistake he made, nor did he try to think it through live in front of the room. He simply threw in the towel. With that, Branch had no choice but to instruct the room to wave goodbye to the latest Vincent. Before the clock struck 7:15, the team was down to four. Then Branch looked at Richard.

"Well, well, well, Mr. Cast. Two time's a charm for you, I see. I hope you are not trying to make a habit out of this now. Before you begin, I wanted you to know that I closed Miller and Goldblatt after you left and because of your error, you will not earn a commission from the sale. Please get up there now and explain your mistake to the team."

While Richard moved to the front of the room, he paused to say a silent thank you to Chamberlain. He knew the message that he was about to deliver was accurate and insightful. Richard would be keeping his job for at least another day, but all he could think about was how he could help Chamberlain. There must be something more he could do for his personal prophet than just be a delivery boy bearing lowfat meals, but that would have to wait. First, he needed to demonstrate his understanding of the events that led to his second mistake.

"Dr. Branch, I understand why you made the decision to withhold the commission, but I will not be apologizing for yesterday's unfortunate error. It only occurred because I had never encountered such a savvy negotiator before, but now that I have experienced the tactic that Dr. Goldblatt used yesterday, I am confident that I will not make the same mistake twice. The mistake I made can be summarized as follows. *It takes a lot of bricks to build a house,* and I should have been more keenly aware that every position taken or demand made by the other party is only one brick, one element inside the complexity of a negotiation. You see, Dr. Branch, I reacted incorrectly when Dr. Goldblatt suggested, in a cryptic yet creative manner, that the only way he'd move forward with the purchase of our solution was if you personally agreed to stay with the company and never sell it to an outside buyer. I tried to convince him, right or wrong, that you would remain our leader for the long haul, but Dr. Goldblatt knew this demand was one you could never agree to. He knew, by your past success in building and selling businesses, that your goal is to grow this company and sell it for a healthy profit. Since his final demand was something he knew you could never agree to, the only way for us to close the sale was to have him accept less than he wanted by offering him additional concessions elsewhere. Something like, *"Dr. Goldblatt, if you will move forward with this purchase with the understanding that Dr. Branch has the right to sell the company at any point in the future, we will offer you an additional 4.36 percent off the price or free maintenance for one year."* Dr. Goldblatt would concede something he never really wanted or needed and would receive an incremental savings on the deal. It was a very smart negotiation tactic that I simply misread. When I committed you to something that you could not do, I immediately put the sale in jeopardy. I did not recognize Dr. Goldblatt's demand as a negotiation tactic, but rather as a true concern that could be overcome by telling him what he wanted to hear. He was better than me yesterday and for that, you are justified in not having me share in the profits from the sale. But it won't happen again. My mantra going forward, when I am in a negotiation is this: ***It takes a lot of bricks to build a house,*** and in the future, I will be more keenly aware that every position taken or demand made by the other party is only one brick, one element inside the complexity of a negotiation."

As if a rerun of an old television show was playing, Dr. Branch sat quietly in his chair and shook his head in confusion. *How can this be? How could Richard pull this off a second time? Why would someone who knew so much and could explain himself so well make such elementary mistakes?* He stood from his seat, wiped the visible confusion from his eyes, and said, "That is correct, Richard. You may keep your job, again."

Branch left the room, and Richard let all the air escape from his lungs. Chamberlain did it again, and Richard realized that without this friendship, he would have never lasted this long at XRQ. He committed right then that the next meal he'd buy for Chamberlain would be served to him by a waitress as the two men sat across from each other at an actual restaurant. No more of this subway floor café nonsense. It was time to treat Chamberlain with the respect and care that he deserved. The only question was which restaurant would allow a filthy homeless man to dine at its establishment?

****

<u>ANALYSIS OF PRINCIPLE #2</u>

It takes a lot of bricks to build a house.

A skilled negotiator must be keenly aware that every position taken or demand made by the other party is only one brick, one element, inside the complexity of a negotiation. Poor Richard! You have to feel bad for the kid because Dr. Branch is setting him up to fail. Richard has been thrust into two important negotiations, but does not have enough experience to succeed. The reality is that only through practice does one truly become a skilled negotiator. Until you sit across the table from someone and learn how to identify their tactics, techniques, and styles and effectively respond to them, all you'll have is book smarts. So the message again is to take the lessons presented here and get out there and negotiate.

Branch, for all his success and intellect, expects too much of his young employees. In Chapter 18 he thinks to himself after Richard's second dissertation, *"How can this be? How could Richard pull this off a second time? Why would someone who knew so much and could explain himself so well make such elementary mistakes?"* The answer is simple. Richard has a basic understanding of negotiation techniques, but does not have knowledge. He has not yet melted the ball of wax on the top of his head. Richard has not practiced the give-and-take of real negotiations enough to avoid making mistakes, nor has he been exposed to the many styles and tactics that are used to gain an advantage in negotiations. But studying the techniques before entering into a negotiation is critical to your success. You must first understand the principles, then be able to identify them when they are in front of you and ultimately be able to respond effectively without hesitation. And the fact that you just read the last few sentences means you agree with me. Right now you are taking time to improve your negotiation skills by broadening your awareness of the various techniques out there. The more you learn about the different tactics, techniques, and styles the other party might use to strengthen his position, the better you'll be able to identify them when they are right in front of you.

Let's explore the technique Dr. Goldblatt used in Chapter 15. Asking for something you don't want or need, only to concede it away in exchange for something you really do want or need, is a fairly common technique, but unfortunately for Richard, it was the first time it was used against him, so he misread the intent. Goldblatt was looking to get something more from Richard or Branch. Let's assume he wanted a better price or maybe free services. By stating his position that the only way he would agree to purchase the *X-Ray Now* solution was if Branch agreed to not sell his company, Goldblatt brought the negotiation to an impasse. Branch would never agree to Goldblatt's terms, but he was also not ready to lose a sale. When Richard lied to Goldblatt and in effect locked Branch into indefinite ownership of the company, Branch knew Richard misread Goldblatt's technique. By Goldblatt conceding his demand and agreeing to make a purchase even if Branch sold the company, Branch had to offer something of value in exchange for Goldblatt accepting less than his stated demand. The result is Branch can sell the company when he wants, he closes his first sale of the *X-Ray Now* solution, and Goldblatt receives an additional incentive just for being a savvy negotiator.

Now let's broaden the discussion of this principle and look at its implications outside the scope of the story. It is critical to the success of the negotiation that both parties never lose sight of the fact that they are negotiating. This is not a simple business discussion. There will always be undisclosed motivations that impact the attitude and behavior of the people involved. There will always be attempts to get a little more and give a little less. Because of that, you must never take what the other party says at face value without at least asking yourself why he said what he said or asked for what he asked for. There should never be a moment that you mentally relax when you are in a negotiation. You must heighten your perception and become a keen observer of human behavior.

It's impossible to predict what negotiation tactic will be used against you, but rest assured that one will be used. It becomes your job to acknowledge and react to tactics used against you to gain an advantage. Pay attention when you negotiate for it is during the negotiation that your ball of wax melts and you turn your understanding into knowledge, into know-how.

So what are other common techniques or tactics used and how do you counter them in a negotiation? It would take volumes to fully answer that question, and many great books have been written on the subject. My advice is to read every one of them. Consume as much information as you possibly can about the art of negotiating. Once you understand the tactics, make sure to identify and respond to them in your negotiations. Although the following list is far from complete, I'll share two of my favorites.

Lies: Don't kid yourself that lies do not rear their ugly head in negotiations. Lies are thrown about all the time, and if they are not refuted or addressed, they quickly become fact, and then those lies can be used as a reference to support one's position. If the other party lies, calling him a liar or calling his statement a lie will do nothing more than damage your relationship and stall the negotiation. My experience has shown me that you only have two options that will result in the fallacy being cast aside. The first response is to ask the other party to substantiate his claims with documented proof that supports his statement.

You might say something like this: "I've never heard that before. Would you help me understand your position more by sharing some of the sources from which you've based your comments?" You immediately put the responsibility on the other party to prove that what he said was true and if he cannot produce a source to support his claim, you say, "Until we can all agree that what you've said is accepted as fact by the general public, let's agree that it won't impact our discussion here." It's a very professional way to help the other party save face and not be embarrassed in front of his peers. The second option is for you to produce documented proof from a mutually agreeable source that supports the opposite position from the other party's claims. If you prove that what the other person has said is not generally accepted by the public, then you once again eliminate the lie from the conversation. But in both cases, you confront the statement, not the person. You do not attack the person with whom you are negotiating. Remember, you're negotiating with someone very much like yourself, and if you were called a liar in front of your peers, how would you react?

Bullying: Some negotiators try to "win" by bullying the other party. It is rarely physical, but names are called, threats are made, unwarranted insults are used, and absurd demands are forced into the negotiation. Identifying bullying is very easy because when it's done to you, you feel horrible. You feel attacked and scared, and thoughts like "get me out of here" run through your head. In my experience, I have found that there is only one effective way to respond when the other person is using the bully technique. The objective here is to get the negotiation back on track so both sides can work toward a mutually beneficial agreement. The professional and mature way to defuse a bully is to stay silent. Do not react at all. Do not defend yourself. Do not utter a sound. Let the other person yell and scream and threaten and insult until he stops. Once he's finished with all his antics, don't move. Don't speak. Just sit there and wait in silence. Silence is so powerful. Not reacting is unsettling to a bully. Bullies thrive on conflict and confrontation, so if you do not give them their lifeblood, they simply go away. Just sit there in silence and wait for the monsoon to pass. If the bully is waiting for you to speak first and has the mindset of "whoever speaks first loses," just wait until you are calm and then say, "Shall we start the meeting?" What this statement does is discount the tirade as having an impact on you or the negotiation. It delivers the message that you are ready to negotiate and have no intention of conducting business any other way than in a mutually respectful and professional manner. Remember, bullies thrive on conflict, so don't fan the fire with a bully. Silence is power here.

Remember to not take the statements, antics, or persuasions of the other party at face value. Do not negotiate in haste. Carefully observe the other party and listen with intent to what he is saying and doing. Question everything, and always remember that a skilled negotiator must be keenly aware that every position taken or demand made by the other party is only one brick, one element, inside the complexity of a negotiation because ***it takes a lot of bricks to build a house.***

****

Chapter 19

As Richard made his way toward the concrete slab that Chamberlain called home, his view was obstructed by a crowd of people staring at the back wall. Some were pointing, but most were laughing. The laughter was not like the cackles inside a comedy club, but rather the type of taunting and belittling laugh you'd hear in the hallways of a junior high school. As Richard pushed his way through the crowd, the spectacle came into view.

Chamberlain was weeping uncontrollably and coddling his guitar as if it were a baby—his long lost baby girl. He gently stroked the long wooden neck, but in his heart he felt her hair. Chamberlain was delusional, and the crowd simply stood by and disgustingly enjoyed their free show. Chamberlain coughed heavily as tears flowed down his cheeks like rain on a dark window. He did what he could to sing the last few words of *Happy Birthday* to the imaginary child in his arms, and the crowd pushed him deeper into his hallucination by clapping and whistling at the poor old man.

Richard was disgusted with the utter lack of humanity in front of him, and before he knew it, he was screaming at the crowd.

"What the hell is the matter with you people!? He is a human being, not some animal here for your amusement. You people are pathetic. Get the hell out of here. Leave. LEAVE NOW!"

Some people cursed back at Richard with expletives and insults about his mother's sexual preference, but mostly, people just continued to watch. It was like a car crash. There is a shameful instinct in people that despite all the tragedy and pain that can result from a fatal car crash, motorists will always slow down to catch a glimpse of the horrors of mangled human flesh. Chamberlain, and now Richard, had become the car crash for all to see. Richard turned his back to the crowd and ran to Chamberlain's side. He placed both hands on Chamberlain's shoulders and gently rocked the old man to try to make him snap out of this other world. Chamberlain's eyes were glossed over as he looked up at Richard, and his blank stare confirmed that he was mentally in a distant place and time.

"It's her birthday today, young man."

"Chamberlain, it's me, Richard. Come on, buddy. What are you talking about?"

"My baby, Estelle. It's her birthday today. She's six-years-old today and she looks just like her momma, don't you think?"

"Chamberlain! Wake up! It's me, Richard."

Richard grabbed Chamberlain harder this time, shook him forcefully, and yelled one last time.

"CHAMBERLAIN. WAKE UP!"

Like a wide angle lens coming into focus, Chamberlain's eyes locked onto Richard, and there was silence. Then, Chamberlain dropped his head to his chest and sobbed. His body heaved, and he clutched his guitar with all his might. Richard kneeled beside him and gently stroked the back of his head. A few minutes passed, and the crowd dissipated because the spectacle had ended. Chamberlain's breathing slowed, and he looked up at Richard. Richard smiled at Chamberlain and said, "May I take you someplace to eat?"

Chamberlain dropped his head in shame and quietly replied, "That would be nice."

Chapter 20

With a touch of sorrow, Cherise asked, "Was the guitar my grandma?"

Richard nodded his head as he said, "I believe so, Cherise."

"I think my grandma would like to know that."

"Will you tell her for me?"

"Yes. I'll tell her just like you told me."

Richard and Cherise continued to make circles around the church as he retold the story. Cherise had not let go of Richard's hand for some time, and he knew that the little girl felt safe with him. She was reliving each moment along with Richard, and as she learned more and more about her great-grandfather, her anger toward Chamberlain began to fade. They stopped by a garden hose to share a sip of cold water, and Cherise begged Richard to continue. The new friends journeyed on, hand in hand, as the giant sun began to set in the North Carolina sky.

Chapter 21

Chamberlain appeared blinded by the sunlight as if it had been years since he'd been above ground. He shielded his eyes with his arm and grimaced as the sun beat down on his fragile frame. With each step, his old bones ached more and more so Richard stood by his side and supported Chamberlain's weight as they trudged along the New York City sidewalks. Richard thought it best to not discuss the hallucination that consumed his friend moments before. It was evident that Chamberlain's faculties were not as sharp as they had been in his youth, and by the way he had clutched his guitar, Richard could only assume it had been too many years since Chamberlain had held his child in his arms. That discussion could wait for another day. The mission before them now was to find a restaurant that would be willing to seat and serve a young professional and his homeless confidant.

At a local bistro, an attractive hostess stood at her post and graciously greeted customers as they entered the posh restaurant for lunch. Her entire demeanor changed the moment she saw the approaching duo. She stepped out from behind her podium and extended a Diana Ross-like stop sign, and her palm landed inches from Richard's face. She blurted the restaurant policy in a condescending tone.

"Excuse me, but we do not serve the homeless at this establishment."

Richard expected as much, but did not want to simply give up and move on without first pressing the issue. The truth of the matter was he was exhausted from carrying Chamberlain's dead weight the last quarter mile.

"Miss, my friend has had a trying day. I have no intention of asking for a handout. I will gladly pay for both our meals."

She hissed back, "Sorry, but he can't come in."

Richard tried again and said, "Miss, please, we are both hungry and just need a place to have a quick bite to eat and then we'll be on our way."

As Richard and the young lady bantered back and forth, Chamberlain stood quietly by and kept his head down. The hostess continued.

"Are you not listening to me? You and your friend are not coming in. Move along before I call the police."

"Come on now. There's no need to call the cops. What if I made it worth your while?"

Richard reached into his pocket and pulled a five dollar bill from his wallet. The hostess rolled her eyes in disgust.

"Are you kidding? Five bucks? Are you trying to insult me? Do you even know what restaurant you are at? Put your money back in your wallet and keep moving or I will call the police."

Richard decided it would be best to continue down the block where he saw a restaurant with patio seating. Perhaps he'd have better luck there. He stuffed the money back into his pocket while Chamberlain shifted the guitar to the right side of his back, and then threw his left arm over Richard's shoulder. They continued along the sidewalk, never once noticing the onlookers or hearing the rude comments as they stepped together in stride. As if a cookie cutter was used to build the outside of all New York City bistros and cafés, another young lady guarded the gate at the second restaurant. Before Richard could open his mouth, the woman offered up a friendly greeting.

"Good afternoon, gentlemen. How may I help you today?"

Richard was taken by surprise. He had been preparing for another confrontation and was already formulating his approach to ask for an outside table on the sidewalk, but this was looking better than he expected.

"Good afternoon to you as well. Table for two, please."

The hostess sighed and said, "Oh, I see. Right, well, I am very sorry, but we have a policy here about not serving the homeless. I'd be happy to place an order to-go for you if you wouldn't mind waiting outside."

"Actually, we would mind. You see, we're both pretty well spent, and we'd just like a place to sit down, relax, and have lunch."

She was uncomfortable with the situation and tried to be as kind as possible when she replied, "Right, but the policy, sir. See, I just can't. I'm sure you understand."

Richard pressed on and asked, "What about a table outside on the patio? You could give us the one all the way at the end where we'll be off to the side, almost like we're not even really there. What do you say?"

"Again, sir, unfortunately, I have to follow the policy or I'll lose my job. Plus, it wouldn't be fair to the other customers. Would you care to place an order to-go? I could put a rush on it for you."

Richard snapped back, "No. We don't want to place an order to-go. We'd like to sit down and eat." Then he tried a more friendly approach and said, "Can I offer you a tip or something to change your mind? I could buy you lunch, too. You could join us. Come on. What do you say?"

The hostess felt bad about the situation, but she was not in a position to accept Richard's offer.

"I'm sorry. We won't be able to serve you today."

Richard shook his head in frustration and said, "Forget it. We'll go someplace else."

The double shut-out left the two men exhausted and hungrier than they expected. The odd couple turned and continued on their journey, when out of nowhere, a golden oasis appeared. The two men stopped, looked at each other, and smiled. There was no chance that they would be turned away here.

As Richard approached the counter, he heard a wonderfully familiar phrase.

"Welcome to McDonald's. May I please take your order?"

Richard sat his friend at a booth near the back of the seating area. Chamberlain began sucking the ketchup out of a stack of packets that had been left on the table. Richard ordered two trays full of food. Salads, burgers, chicken, fish, fries, apple pies, onion rings, soda, water, and milkshakes. By the time he returned to the table, Chamberlain had ripped into seven ketchup packets, successfully swallowing the contents of five, while the other two landed on his chin and chest. When the trays hit the table, Chamberlain's eye nearly popped out of their sockets. He took a deep breath, loosened the button on his pants, rolled up his sleeves, and forgot all about his healthy food requirements. Chamberlain ate and ate and ate. With every swallow another pound of stress fell from his back. After twenty minutes of non-stop chewing, Chamberlain finally pushed the tray away from his belly, sat back, clasped his hands behind his head, and let out a thunderous belch. The two men shared a hardy laugh as onlookers tried to ignore the bizarre interaction between Richard and Chamberlain. Despite having shared an entire lunch together, neither of the men had uttered a word. They simply took in the silence and relaxed. Finally, Chamberlain leaned forward and spoke.

"Richard, if you were paying attention today, you would have realized that you made another negotiation mistake. Were you paying attention?"

Richard was lost.

"I guess I wasn't paying attention. What are you talking about?"

Chamberlain felt alive for the first time in decades. He finally had someone to connect with. Someone to help him feel human again. Someone to help him down the path of redemption from his tragic past. He smiled and continued.

"Richard, in less than five minutes, you failed miserably at two negotiations that you could have never won in the first place. The worst part of it all was that you failed without even knowing you were in a negotiation."

Richard was confused and said, "What are you talking about?"

Chamberlain leaned in and said, "I'm talking about your conversations with the ladies at the two restaurants. I'm talking about your request for a table, both inside and on the patio. I'm talking about the fact that you created your own failure without ever even understanding why. Let me ask you something. At the first restaurant, when you asked the girl for a table, was there anything you could have said to her to make her say yes?"

Richard thought about it and then replied, "No. We were not going to get a table there."

"Correct. And at the second place, could you have done anything different to get us a table?"

"No, I don't think so."

"Correct again, Richard. You could not have done anything to get us a table and here's why. In the world there are certain laws that will always exist. These laws can never be changed, like the law of gravity. It doesn't matter how hard you throw the ball up into the air, it will always come back down. Even a child's balloon will eventually pop and float back to earth. So there is nothing you can do to change the law of gravity, and if you spend your days trying to find a way, all you'll do is hurt your arm foolishly throwing that ball. You just have to realize that you can't change certain laws in the world, and sometimes those types of laws exist in a negotiation, but are presented as the other person's position. You must realize that when you are confronted with an immovable law or position, you can't change it, and you'll damage any potential outcome of the negotiation if you try to force the other person to break his law. Identifying when the other person's position is one of his immovable laws is a difficult thing to do, but in order to be successful in a negotiation, you must *recognize when you are negotiating with gravity*."

Richard had a confused look on his face, so Chamberlain continued.

"Let me try to help you understand this one more clearly. When you made your first request for a table, you forced the hostess to stand by her unbreakable law. Restaurants have rules for people like me, and those rules will never go away. There was nothing you could have said or done to make her change her position. Your five dollar tip was insignificant, but even if she wanted the money, she was never going to break the law of the restaurant. You did not offer any other alternatives, and even if you did, she was never going to let us in, so we left and there was no deal. At the second restaurant, she was not willing to let us in either, but offered an alternative, a concession on your part. Had you taken her up on her offer to place a to-go order, you would have been conceding your position, and you were not ready to do that. You chose to demand a seat, offered nothing she could have accepted because you were negotiating with an unbreakable law, and the result again was the same as the first: no deal. That's twice you failed to recognize you were negotiating with gravity. Finally, you conceded your position of wanting to take me to an expensive restaurant when you brought me here. Let me give you another example. Do you have any brothers or sisters?"

"No. I'm an only child, Chamberlain."

"OK, then. What about a dog? Do you have a dog, Richard?"

"Yes. Well, he's at home with my parents now, but yes, we have a dog."

Chamberlain smiled and said, "Then let's use the dog. What's the dog's name, by the way?"

"Peanut."

"And Richard, what kind of a dog is Peanut?"

Richard didn't know where Chamberlain was going with this, but he said, "He's a Great Dane. Why?"

"One of those horse-size dogs?"

"Yes, he's pretty big. Why are you asking me this, Chamberlain?"

"Richard, if he's a big dog, why did you name him Peanut? That's a small dog's name."

"I named him when he was a puppy. My parents knew he was going to grow into a giant dog, but I had no clue at the time. They told me to name him something like Rex or King, but I liked Peanut."

Satisfied, Chamberlain continued.

"Let me ask you something about Peanut. Do you love your dog?"

"Of course I love him, Chamberlain."

"No, Richard. I mean, do you really love your dog? Some people just ain't dog people, but they have dogs because families get dogs. So, are you one of those people or do you love your dog?"

Richard did not have to think about that one. He answered right away.

"I love my dog. I picked him out. I paid for him with the money I earned working at my family's store. He slept in my bed with me until I left for college. I love my dog. Why?"

Chamberlain smirked as he asked, "Can I have him?"

"What do you mean can you have him?"

"It's a simple question, Richard. Can I have Peanut?"

Confused, Richard asked, "How would I give him to you, Chamberlain? Where would you keep him? How would you feed him?"

Chamberlain became stern with Richard and said, "That's not what I'm asking you. I just want to know if I can have him."

"No, you can't have my dog."

"Richard. What if I told you I won't help you anymore? What if I said, I will not give you the answers to your questions ever again and you'd have to figure out your negotiation mistakes on your own. Could I have Peanut then?"

Richard stopped to think about how that would impact his career, but then said, "No. I'd figure it out on my own."

"And what if I said, if you give me Peanut, I'd live for another ten years, but if you don't, I'd die next week. Could I have your dog then, Richard?"

"Chamberlain, don't talk like that. Why would you say something like that?"

"Just answer the question, Richard. If you don't give me the dog, I die. Will you give me the dog?"

Richard was uncomfortable and said, "I don't see how one thing has anything to do with the other."

Chamberlain hit the table with his fist and said, "Richard. Just answer the question. If you don't give me the dog, I am going to die. Will you give me the dog?"

Richard paused as he battled his guilt. He loved that dog more than most people love their siblings, but how could he not trade Peanut to save a human life, especially Chamberlain's? He could not look his mentor in the eyes when he replied.

"No. I can't trade my dog. I'm sorry. I just can't."

Chamberlain softened his tone and said, "Could I come visit him, Richard? If I can come visit him, I might live for two more years. What do you say to that?"

"Of course you could come visit my dog. What's your point?"

Chamberlain leaned back, smiled, and winked at Richard.

"Richard. My point is this: I was negotiating with gravity. There was nothing I could have said to make you give me your dog. Even though your dog could give me an extra ten years of life, I was not going to get him, but I was not willing to die next week, so I recognized that I was negotiating with one of your immovable laws or positions. I chose to reduce my request and was willing to only live for two more years when you said I could visit Peanut. Remember Richard, you must *recognize when you are negotiating with gravity.*"

Richard smiled back at Chamberlain. The lesson had hit home, and Richard completely understood what Chamberlain was trying to teach him.

"I do have one question for you, Chamberlain."

"What's that, son?"

"If I had a brother or a sister, was I going to have to give them to you too in order to save your life?"

"Yes. Except they would have given me only one more year to live. Dogs are much easier to care for than humans."

Chamberlain grabbed the chocolate milkshake off the table and smiled as he slowly sipped the cold drink. Richard was amazed as his head flooded with questions. *How had Chamberlain turned a walk to lunch into an incredible lesson in negotiations? How could a man who knew so much about business be homeless? Why would Chamberlain choose to stay on the streets when all he needed to do was shower, shave, buy a suit, and go on a job interview?* Richard thought it best to not pursue that conversation, but knew that he'd bring it up one day soon. For now, it was time for Richard to head back home to prepare for another day at work.

"Chamberlain, I can't thank you enough. You have given me more in the past few days than I could have ever imagined. You have become my mentor, and I respect you for all you have done for me. I don't want to insult you by offering anything more than what you asked for when we made our pact, but if you need something, anything—food, money or shelter—I need you to ask. I need you to put your pride aside and ask me for help and I will help you, Chamberlain. I will help you."

Chamberlain welled up with emotion. Richard had touched his soul, and he was visibly moved. He was ashamed of what he had become, but asking this boy for anything more than a meal every once in a while was out of the question. In his gut, he felt he did not deserve even that bit of generosity. After all that had happened to his family and the families of the men and women who worked in the factory, Chamberlain believed his self-imposed life of poverty was a burden worth bearing to preserve his father's good name. He took Richard's hand and held it between his two calloused palms.

"Richard, you are a good man. A man I am proud to call my friend. Our pact is binding and cannot be changed. It shall remain as agreed. No more. No less. If you don't mind, I'd like to be alone for a while."

Richard desperately wanted to help Chamberlain more than he had, but it was clear that Chamberlain would not allow that to happen. So Richard stood, gathered the garbage from the table and placed his hand on Chamberlain's shoulder.

"Be well, my friend. I will see you soon."

As Richard walked out of the restaurant, he turned back to make sure Chamberlain was all right.   Richard's heart cried out as he watched the old man clutch his guitar close to his chest and stroke the long wooden neck.

"Happy Birthday, sweetheart.   Papa loves you."

****

ANALYSIS OF PRINCIPLE #3

Recognize when you are negotiating with gravity.

The lesson here was covered extensively in Chamberlain's explanation to Richard, but there is enough going on with this principle that it deserves a bit more discussion. One quick point to bring up before we begin. Every interaction or conversation you have could potentially be a negotiation. If you are serious about mastering this craft, always stay "tuned in" when you are involved in a verbal exchange. Never miss an opportunity to develop your skills. Richard viewed his interactions with the hostesses as nothing more than a conversation and missed two opportunities to practice his negotiation skills. Look for opportunities outside of work to practice what you've learned. Negotiate with your spouse about where to go for dinner or what movie to see. Try a few techniques out on your kids when they ask to stay up for an extra hour or demand more money for their allowance. Bargain for a better price or extra goodies when you're at the department store. Practice, practice, practice. Never miss the chance to improve your skills.

This principle is complex, and people with diverse negotiation experiences might interpret it differently than how it is explained here. This once again proves the point that we all approach negotiations from our unique perspectives. In a moment, I'll share some additional thoughts about recognizing when you are negotiating with gravity, but I thought it would be interesting to explore two additional principles that some of you might have thought about while reading the story. The first interpretation is the concept that when you want what the other person has more than they want what you have, you have to ask yourself if you are prepared to move off your position and make concessions to get what you want. The second is when your position or demand backs the other party into a corner with no way out and they refuse to relinquish their position, there can only be two results: no deal or a concession from you.

Let's first look at potential concessions you might make if you want what the other person has more than they want what you have. On the surface, Richard's encounters with the two hostesses might appear to fit this theory, but what was really going on in the story was much deeper. Regardless, this interpretation of the story is too important to pass by without diving into it. The key here is preparation. Before entering into any negotiation, you must know what you want, what you need, and what you are willing to concede before you call off the negotiation and walk away. If you want what the other party has more than they want what you have, you must know what you're willing to part with to get what you want and where your breaking point is. That is the point at which you know you'll walk away without getting what they have because it simply means you'd have to give away too much of what you have. If you fail to prepare and clearly answer these questions before you begin negotiating, you will likely end up negotiating from your emotions rather than your entire being, and you might just end up giving away more than you planned. Prepare. Prepare. Prepare. I can't say it enough.

The second interpretation of the story that you might have considered is this: When your position or demand backs the other party into a corner with no way out, and he refuses to relinquish his position, there can only be two results: no deal or a concession from you. Picture yourself walking down a dark street, late at night, in a bad part of town. You're by yourself and feeling concerned for your safety. You turn down an alley that you think is a cut-through street, but it turns out to be a dead end. When you turn around to walk back to the main street, there is a man in a trench coat standing in front of you, blocking your way. What do you do? How do you feel? At this moment you are literally backed into a corner with no way out. Who is in the position of power? Obviously, it is the man blocking your way. And what are your options? Beyond begging the man to let you go without harm, you really do not hold many options. Unlike Richard's negotiation with the hostesses where they did not concede their positions of not granting entrance to the restaurants, when you are physically backed into a corner, it is common to move from position to concession quickly. Moving from "Please don't hurt me, just let me go" to "You can have all of my money, just don't hurt me," to "I'll do whatever you want, just don't hurt me" can happen in an instant. Now shift focus for a moment and think about a negotiation in the business world. The objective of any negotiation that is being done in good faith should be to create a mutually beneficial agreement. If you agree with me, then how does making demands that back the other party into a corner help you achieve that goal? The answer is, it doesn't. When someone is backed into a corner, his intellect is overpowered by his instinct to survive and his focus shifts to self preservation, not to negotiating fairly. No lasting business relationship can truly be developed when one party's position or demand backs the other side into a corner and forces the negotiation in a direction away from that of a mutually beneficial agreement. So use your demands and positions carefully since it's possible that through your demands, you'll steer the negotiation away from an agreement.

To take this principle one step further, we should start at the beginning of the negotiation planning session. To expand upon what I mentioned above, before entering into any negotiation, it is your duty to prepare. Part of the planning process requires you to develop a clear understanding of what you want versus what you need, what you are willing to give up to get what you want and need, when you will make your concessions, and finally when you will walk away with no deal because the terms are not in the best interest of both parties. If you enter into a negotiation blindly and have not prepared, you increase your chances of getting far less than you want or need and giving away much more than you can afford to part with. Preparation is paramount to the success of every negotiation.

In Chapter 8 Dr. Branch challenges his staff to expound upon the notion that "The path from position to concession is a slippery slope." Mark Kramer, the pint-sized Wharton graduate, states, "If you have not properly prepared for your sales call, which includes many topics that you have covered today as well as others I'm sure you will discuss with us over the next few weeks, you weaken your ability to position your superior products and services to your customers. Once you are standing on unstable ground, you risk offering a series of financial, technical, and business concessions, or in layman's terms, customer giveaways, in order to avoid the loss of the sale. Therefore, you must prepare for all sales calls, stand firm in your position that you offer a quality product, and do not simply concede your position of price, terms, and deliverables just to close the sale." Mark was 100 percent accurate here in terms of answering Dr. Branch's question, but there is a lot more to discuss when talking about positions and concessions in relationship to Chamberlain's Third Principle.

Assuming you've prepared well and developed a list of all your wants and what you would be willing to concede away to get what you need, then answer this question. Does conceding a want to get to a need impact the other party's perception of the rest of your demands? Asked differently, if you make a demand and then back away from it, do you then give the other party reason to believe that all your demands are negotiable? The answer is maybe. It depends upon the demand itself within the context of the negotiation, when it's conceded, and what you get in exchange for the concession. The point here is to not be frivolous with your positions or concessions. Don't overload your negotiation plan with demands that you don't really want and concede them away in order to get what you need. That technique only works when it's used in moderation. If you ask for ten things and concede eight away in exchange for the two you really need, you've wasted a lot of time and revealed that you would have been willing to take advantage of the other party had he not been a savvy enough negotiator to get you to give up the eight silly wants. Once the other party questions the importance of your demands because you've conceded them too fast or accepted something of lesser value in exchange for the concession, he will begin to ask himself if it's possible to make you concede all of your demands.

The reason why Richard could not gain entrance into the two restaurants was because Richard and the hostesses both had true needs, not frivolous wants, that they were willing or able to part with. Richard was negotiating with gravity. The rules that the hostesses followed could not be changed no matter what Richard said or did. If you offer a take-it or leave-it demand that is in direct conflict with the other party's immovable position, he won't back down, and you will have brought the negotiation to an impasse. To get beyond that impasse, the choice of what to do next belongs to you. You can walk away because you feel strongly that if you take any less than what you demand, you would be conceding a true need. Or you could reevaluate your demand and determine if it's a need or just a want. In Richard's case, he had a true need to eat with his mentor at a restaurant. He was not willing to order food to-go because he felt Chamberlain deserved the right to be treated like any other human being. So he stood his ground and walked away until he found a place that would fulfill his need. Granted, Richard adjusted it slightly by moving from a New York City corner bistro to McDonald's as Chamberlain pointed out to him, but his need to treat his mentor with respect was too important to abandon his cause all together. Although Richard did not succeed in his objective to dine with Chamberlain at a fancy restaurant, he now knows what it feels like to hold onto a need and not concede it away. The ball of wax on top of his head has begun to melt.

The real challenge is learning how to identify when you are negotiating with gravity. Even if the other person says, "This point is not negotiable," it still may be a position he is willing to concede away if you offer something he needs. So how do you determine when the other person's position truly is something he will not part with? The answer lies in the broader scope of the negotiation. It starts with the foundation of a trusted relationship where the two parties are negotiating in good faith for a mutually beneficial agreement. Through your relentless questioning, you will soon discover the other person's needs versus his wants. You might consider using the Potential Concession technique to see if he is willing to concede, but if the other party still does not move off his position after you offer to concede what you perceive to be an inequitable amount in his favor, then it might just be time to assume his position is a rule or a law that he cannot break. Regardless, it's important that you never push so hard that you damage the relationship.

Here is an example to illustrate the process for determining if you are negotiating with gravity. Let's pretend that you are negotiating to purchase a house that is listed for $500,000 and the seller has stated that the 1910 Steinway grand piano that has been in his family for three generations does not come with the house. After doing your research, you know that the piano sells for about $80,000, and you would love to own it. By presenting a **Third Party Potential Concession**, you can distance yourself from the negotiation, which will alter how the seller responds. Perhaps you say, "Mr. Jones, the Steinway grand piano is a beautiful work of art. I know you've stated that the piano does not come with the house, but what would you do if the next person that walked through the door offered to pay you $900,000 cash for your home today if you included the piano? That would be like offering you $200,000 for the piano and $200,000 above the asking price of your home. If someone presented you an offer like that, would you consider including the piano with the house?"

From a purely financial perspective, the offer to pay $400,000 more than the asking price is not equitable for the goods being exchanged and this "out-of-alignment" helps create a safe place for the seller to ponder the offer because he knows it's unrealistic that anyone would make that offer in reality. Additionally, by presenting this offer as if it were coming from a third party, you remove yourself from the negotiation and the seller is given the chance to safely consider the proposal in some imaginary world as opposed to within the structure of the real negotiation you are having with him. So if the seller says yes to this farfetched proposal, you know you are not negotiating with gravity. The piano is for sale, and it's just a matter of finding the right offer to present to the seller that will tip the scale. If, however, the seller will still not part with the piano even if offered something far beyond his asking price, it would be safe to assume that you are negotiating with gravity and that the piano, which is likely a priceless heirloom that the seller expects to be kept in the family for years to come, will never be sold with the house.

So remember, preparation is critical to the success of the negotiation. Be strategic and considerate when building your wants, needs, and concessions. When in the negotiation, state your position respectfully, make your demands carefully, offer your concessions cautiously, and always strive to ***recognize when you are negotiating with gravity.***
****

Chapter 22

The next morning as Richard rode the elevator up to the office, his cell phone buzzed, announcing the arrival of a new text message. He flipped the phone open, and as he read the message, a shot of adrenaline ran through his body.

Stuck on train. Start SS mtg w/o me. Dr.A.B.

Richard snapped his phone shut and used the elevator's inside door as a makeshift mirror to recheck his appearance. He knew that today's meeting was going to be another test, but this unexpected change of events filled him with both excitement and nausea. He knew the moment the doors opened he'd be running the show until Dr. Branch arrived.

The lights signaled the arrival at the eleventh floor, the bell chimed, and the elevator doors slid open. It was Richard's time to shine. Dr. Branch had passed him the reins that morning, and he mentally prepared himself for the meeting as he walked down the hallway. He focused on positive thoughts and the lessons he'd learned from Branch and Chamberlain. Richard was ready. He would not make a mistake today.

When Richard entered the lobby, he was immediately greeted by Shilpa Subramanian, the Chief Technology Officer of one of India's leading MRI facilities headquartered in Bangalore. Shilpa was an elegant woman with dark brown eyes and smooth olive skin that made her appear much younger than her true age. She was an engineer by trade, schooled in England, and grew her experience over a thirty-year career as a senior executive at a number of high tech companies throughout Europe. Three years ago she returned home to her native India to help her father realize a vision of launching MRI facilities that offered medical services for the less fortunate throughout their homeland. Ms. Subramanian was all business and had no intention of wasting her time on formalities. The moment Richard made eye contact, Shilpa went to work.

"Good morning, Mr. Cast. My name is Shilpa Subramanian. Dr. Branch reached me on my mobile to inform me he was unexpectedly delayed on a broken train and that you could answer all my questions until his arrival. Is this true?"

"Ms. Subramanian, it is a pleasure to meet you this morning. And yes, of course, I will certainly be able to assist you with any questions you may have. Dr. Branch also communicated his delay to me, and I am well prepared to speak with you today."

"Excellent. Please bring me a hot cup of chamomile tea with milk and sugar, and then we shall begin."

"Of course. Would you please make your way into the conference room to your left and I'll be right in with your tea."

Shilpa turned sharply and headed straight for the conference room. Once the door closed behind her, Richard took off down the corridor to the break room where he whipped up a cup of tea, grabbed a stack of biscuits, and threw them onto a plate. Without missing a beat, he grabbed the milk, the sugar, and a handful of napkins as he bolted back down the hall to the conference room. Before pushing the door open with his foot, he took one settling breath and then headed inside.

Unbeknownst to Richard and Shilpa, as they began their conversation, Dr. Branch secretly stood in his dark office and watched the meeting through the one-way mirror on the wall between the two rooms. Branch had installed the four-by-six half-silvered picture window and an audio feed for this exact purpose: to monitor the progress of his sales staff. He was careful to ensure that the lighting in both rooms was just right to maintain the illusion of a mirror on the conference room side. The window installer demonstrated that it was not truly a one-way mirror, but rather a piece of glass with a special silver-plating on only one side. When the room with the silver-plating was lit and the other room was dark, the treated side reflected the light and acted as a mirror. When both rooms were fully lit, you can see right through the glass like a regular window. So Branch stood silently in the darkness and watched the meeting unfold.

There had never been a delay on the train that morning. In fact, Branch had taken the early train and arrived at the office before 6:00 a.m. This staged delay was all part of the training process to groom young Richard into a negotiation expert. Dr. Branch knew Richard had something the others didn't, and his training needed to ramp up fast in order for Branch to reach his larger goals. He did not care one bit about the mistakes that Richard made in the previous meetings. His concern had always been in the ability of his sales staff to clearly articulate the core issues and subsequent fallout from their errors. Once articulated correctly, it was Branch's experience that the mistake would not happen again. Richard had an amazing ability to get right to the root of the mistake and explain it in such a way that Branch knew Richard fundamentally grasped the art of negotiation. So he stood quietly in the darkness and secretly watched his star pupil in action.

Back in the conference room, Richard answered Ms. Subramanian's technical questions about the software, hardware, and infrastructure requirements. They covered such topics as network bandwidth, IP security, routing protocols, product lead times, site surveys, installation, customs, application upgrades, technical support, onsite support, training, and many others. Richard proved himself as an expert in all aspects of the business. He established the true value of the *X-Ray Now* solution and skillfully handled every objection she made, but now the conversation was about to move toward crafting a proposal that would meet, and hopefully exceed, Ms. Subramanian's needs and expectations.

"Mr. Cast, I am quite impressed. You have made me feel very comfortable with your solution and I would now like to draft the details of an agreement."

Richard nearly jumped out of his skin. He was about to close his first deal. Richard wished that Chamberlain could be here to see him in action. Chamberlain would be so proud of how well he'd done. Richard had surprised Ms. Subramanian with his expertise and simultaneously impressed himself with how far he'd come. Richard excused himself from the table in order to pull a contract packet from the closet in the back of the room. As he walked away from the table, Richard realized he just thought about Chamberlain before Dr. Branch. In fact, he had not thought about Dr. Branch once during the meeting. That put a smile on his face. Richard returned to the table with the contract and placed it in front of Shilpa. As Richard sat down, he felt a great sense of pride and accomplishment. He had done well.

"Ms. Subramanian, what we have here is our standard contract language. I'd like to go through this with you now and begin to customize the pricing, the deliverables, and the terms of our agreement so that they may best meet your needs."

Before the final word was out of Richard's mouth, the conference room door flew open with such force that a gust of wind blew the contract right off the table. Richard watched the papers float from side to side as they drifted to the ground. As the contract lay to rest on the floor by Shilpa's feet, Richard's heart sunk to his gut, and he felt the fog of Dr. Branch spill into the room. Even though Branch had not spoken a word, his negativity choked Richard, and he knew that he somehow failed again.

"Good morning, Ms. Subramanian. I am Dr. Alan Branch. I'm terribly sorry for being late. It is a true pleasure to have you here with us today. I trust that Richard has treated you well this morning?"

"Why yes, Dr. Branch. Excellent to make your acquaintance. I must say that Richard has been wonderfully helpful."

Dr. Branch manufactured a smile and said, "I am pleased to hear that. If I could borrow Richard for just a moment, I would greatly appreciate it."

"Of course, please, take your time. I'm content to sip my tea for a bit."

"Thank you so much, Ms. Subramanian. Richard, may I speak with you outside for a moment?"

Richard could hardly lift his body from his seat, but he used whatever strength he had left in his arms and legs to push himself up. Dr. Branch held the door open for Richard and shook his head in disappointment ever so slightly as Richard passed. Once he cleared the door, Richard simply continued walking without even looking back. He headed straight out of the office and right down the hallway to the elevator. By the time the bell rang and the elevator doors opened, Dr. Branch was already inside the conference room with Ms. Subramanian explaining that Richard was urgently called away to their manufacturing facility. Richard had failed again. He was three for three. Or rather, zero for three, and once again he had absolutely no idea what went wrong. It was getting to be ridiculous, and Chamberlain was going to reach a point where he was not going to be able to help anymore. Food and friendship would only go so far. Every now and then, you have to be truthful in your self-evaluation to determine if you are any good, and right now, Richard was questioning his abilities. But there was one man who could fix things and that was Chamberlain Zacharias Taylor III. So Richard stopped by the corner deli once more and grabbed two egg sandwiches, a few oranges, and two cups of black coffee. He replayed the morning's events in his head as he made his way to the subway. The only thing that really stood out as strange was how Dr. Branch appeared just as the contract came out. It was like he was clairvoyant. Richard just chalked it up as an innate gift that Branch possessed, but it was a strange coincidence.

Chapter 23

As if they had been friends for decades, the moment Chamberlain laid eyes on Richard from across the platform, he called out, "Richard!"

And Richard replied on cue, "Chamberlain!"

Then together, they both said in harmony, "Richard Chamberlain!" and laughed. The banter had become like a verbal version of a secret handshake. It was meaningless in and of itself, but was their private way of acknowledging the bond between them. The happiness quickly subsided as Richard approached, and Chamberlain saw the concern in Richard's eyes.

"Richard, you don't look well this morning, son. It's awfully early for you to be seeking my guidance. What did you do now?"

"Chamberlain, I must be the worst salesman in the country. I have no idea what just happened. I had everything under control. I said everything right. I did not do anything wrong."

Chamberlain smiled and said, "Then why are you here?"

"Because I... because I... I don't know. I have no clue what I did wrong again and that's the problem. I never know what I do wrong. I don't care about making the mistakes. I just care that I can't figure them out on my own. It's not like you're going to be with me forever. I'm going to have to learn how to do this myself one day, but Chamberlain, I'm stuck. I need your help again."

"And so you shall receive my help, as long as the contents of that white bag in your hand make their way to my mouth."

Realizing that he was still holding the breakfast, Richard said, "Oh. Sorry about that. I'm going on and on about me and I forgot about the food. I'm sorry. I got us some egg sandwiches this morning. A little fattening with the cheese and butter, but I needed something good."

As Chamberlain unwrapped the sandwich, he said, "I'll manage. So, tell me son, what happened today?"

Richard retold the morning events as Chamberlain devoured his breakfast in three bites. Then Richard watched Chamberlain do something he'd never seen before. Chamberlain picked up one of the oranges and bit into it like it was an apple. His broken teeth ripped away at the entire orange, peel and all. As Chamberlain's chipped incisors penetrated the fruit's flesh, pieces of the bitter rind went flying through the air. A few specks even landed on Richard's pants so he brushed them away as he sat down next to his mentor. Decades on the unforgiving New York City streets had taught Chamberlain how to live on sustenance that most people would discard. It was a sad reminder that despite all his knowledge and wisdom, Chamberlain was homeless and had been turned somewhat savage over the years. Chamberlain washed the entire orange down with the hot coffee and then grabbed another orange and dropped it inside the belly of his guitar. The battered wooden vessel had become his companion, his daughter, his knapsack, and his protector. He never let go of it and almost always held it close to his heart.

Chamberlain belched and then said, "Tell me more about this Shilpa woman. Tell me about who she is, where she comes from, who she works for. You're leaving something out."

Richard shared Shilpa's background with Chamberlain. He talked about her college education. He mentioned her international work experience, and just after Richard mentioned the MRI company with Shilpa's father, Chamberlain let out a shout.

"Ah ha! That's where you failed, my boy. It is now clear why your boss had you leave today."

Richard was stunned and said, "Why? What do you mean, Chamberlain? What did I do?"

"Richard, this mistake is easy to avoid by asking one simple question before you begin the negotiation. Do you know what that one question is?"

"No, I don't know. Please tell me."

"Come on now, my boy. Think. What could you have asked your customer that would have helped you today and stopped your boss from throwing you out again?"

Richard took a deep breath and settled down. His mind was racing, but he knew Chamberlain was right. He had to try to figure this out on his own. Just having Chamberlain spoonfeed him the answer was not going to help him in the long term. So he cleared his mind. *What could I have asked Shilpa today? What am I missing?*

"Okay, Chamberlain. What if I asked her this? 'Do you have the budget set aside to make this purchase?' Is that what you are looking for?"

Chamberlain shook his head and said, "No. That's not correct. Good try, though. Keep going. I'm looking for one specific question."

Richard thought some more and guessed again.

"What about this one? 'If I meet all your needs, are you prepared to purchase our product today?' Is that it?"

"You're getting warmer, son. Keep going."

"Come on, Chamberlain. Just tell me."

"Richard, you're almost there. Indulge an old man. Try one more time. Remember, it's a question you should have asked before you started negotiating."

Richard did not want to take the easy way out. He truly wanted to solve this mistake on his own, but he was stuck. It was embarrassing enough to be thrown out of the office by Dr. Branch, but now he felt incompetent in front of Chamberlain. Putting his pride aside, he tried one more time.

"What about this one? 'Before we begin, do you have any specific requirements that need to be met in order for us to reach an agreement today?' Is that it? Is that the one question you were thinking of?"

"Not bad. Not bad at all, Richard. It's not the right question for the error you made today, but it's not a bad question to ask. The one question that you should have asked to avoid today's mistake is this: 'If we come to an agreement today, do you have the authority to sign the contract?' Or put another way, 'Once we reach an agreement, is there anyone else who needs to approve the details or are you the final authority here?' You see, Richard, you were negotiating with the wrong person. You missed it. Your customer was setting you up to offer as much as you could today, then she was going to say she needed to check with Daddy. And, of course, when Daddy flies all the way to America, you can bet your momma that you'll be offering more concessions to close the deal."

Richard's jaw dropped as he thought out loud.

"You're saying that Shilpa was acting like she was going to make the purchase and then once I gave away a discount or other concessions, she was going to stop and tell me she had to ask her father for permission?"

"Not so much permission, but yes, she was going to stop after you gave away whatever it was you were planning on giving away today.

She was going to see how much she could get from you and then have her father make you give away more at the next meeting. Richard, ***you have to know who's cast in the play*** because unknowingly negotiating with someone who is not the final authority will likely result in your offering additional concessions when the ultimate decision maker arrives. You see, we all play a role in a negotiation. Sometimes we're an extra that walks on stage to deliver the main character a note, and other times we play the lead role with all the great dialogue. You have to realize that the people in a negotiation are like actors in a play, and you must know which character you are talking to. If you don't find out what role the other person is playing you might end up talking to the wrong character. As a negotiator, it's your responsibility to always find out up-front if the person you are negotiating with is the one making the decision."

Richard shook his head in amazement and said, "Unbelievable. I never even saw that coming. She set me up good today. I wonder what happened after I left. I wonder if Dr. Branch closed the deal."

"Probably not. Most likely he set up a call for another day."

Richard thought about it and said, "Yeah. You're probably right, Chamberlain. Okay. I have to get home now. I have to figure out how I'm going to explain this one to the team tomorrow."

"Just tell them the way I told you and you'll be just fine, son."

"Thank you, Chamberlain. Thank you for everything."

"Richard, my boy, thank you as well. You've helped make an old man feel young again."

Richard boarded the next train and headed home. Chamberlain stretched his legs out and watched the people in the subway come and go. He reached inside his guitar to make sure the orange was still there. He knew that if he was unable to find any food later that day, at least he'd have something to eat for supper, and that put a smile on his face. He closed his eyes and drifted off to sleep.

Chapter 24

Richard fundamentally understood the importance of qualifying the person you were negotiating with, but wanted to make sure he retold Chamberlain's message perfectly. So Richard spent over three hours planning exactly what he was going to tell Dr. Branch the next day. Exhausted from preparing for his third dissertation and distracted by his newfound sense of confidence, Richard accidentally drifted off to sleep without setting his alarm, and when his internal clock woke him the next morning, he was already thirty minutes behind schedule. Richard grabbed yesterday's crumpled suit from the hamper and threw it on while he ran out of his building screaming for a cab. He found a taxi at the corner of his block and told the driver there was a $10 tip waiting for him if he could get Richard to the office before 7:00 a.m. The driver nodded, told Richard to buckle his seatbelt, and then slammed his foot down on the gas pedal, leaving a pungent cloud of burnt rubber behind.

At 6:59 a.m., Richard handed the driver the fare plus the $10 tip and hopped out of the cab. He ran inside the building and jumped in the elevator just before the doors closed. It was 7:03 a.m. when the elevator opened on the eleventh floor. Richard bolted down the hallway and came crashing into the conference room. Dr. Branch had not yet arrived so Richard tucked his shirt in, straightened his tie, hand-combed his hair, and sat down at his familiar spot in the front row.

Just as Richard's heart rate fell back to normal, Dr. Branch came through the door, and a chill shot up Richard's spine. It was a strange reaction. Almost Pavlovian, but despite his body's auto-response to Branch's entrance, he knew there was nothing to worry about today. Chamberlain had prepared him well. Richard knew the routine, so he took center stage. Branch sat down in Richard's vacated seat and simply motioned for him to begin. Richard couldn't get a read on Dr. Branch that morning. Usually he was a fireball, but today, he almost seemed eager to listen to Richard speak. Although these moments were brought about by Richard's incompetence in front of the customer, the team all looked forward to his commentary. He may be the one making the most mistakes, but he did so because he put himself out there to fail. He was a risk taker, and the others now respected him for it. Richard took a breath and began.

"Shilpa Subramanian pulled a fast one on me yesterday. Dr. Branch, you did the right thing again by having me leave. I was so proud of how well I positioned XRQ with Ms. Subramanian that I got caught up in the moment. It never even dawned on me to ask her one simple, but vitally important question. And that question is this: 'If we come to an agreement today, do you have the authority to sign the contract?' I didn't ask that question and that's where I failed."

Dr. Branch shook his head in disbelief again. Richard continued.

"You see, Shilpa was not the decision maker. Her father back in India is the one that will say yes or no to the purchase. Shilpa was just the set-up man, or woman in this case, trying to get me to give away as much as possible up-front, and then her father would try to negotiate more out of the deal at the next meeting. It is absolutely critical to qualify the person you are negotiating with before the negotiations begin, or at least before you start to offer any concessions. It is certainly fine to negotiate with the middle-man, but you must go into the negotiation knowing exactly what his role is so that you may carefully maneuver through any concessions you plan to offer. You see, the people in a negotiation are like actors in a play. Some don't speak at all, some are extras with a few lines, and some are cast as the leads with all the good speeches. The point here is that a negotiation, like a play, has cast members playing different roles and those roles are critical to understand before the dialogue begins. In summary, ***you have to know who's cast in the play*** because unknowingly negotiating with someone who is not the final authority will likely result in your offering additional concessions when the ultimate decision maker arrives."

As he had done before, Richard wowed the team with his analysis, and while Dr. Branch sat silent in his chair, the others offered up a well-deserved round of applause. Branch remained seated longer than normal, and the fact that he had not yet told Richard that he could keep his job became obvious to the group. Something was wrong. Dr. Branch was not satisfied. The room became still, and everyone settled back into their seats. Richard stood frozen at the front of the room. Branch was picking at his nails a bit as if he was lost in thought, and then he challenged Richard.

"Explain something to me, Cast. Do you think you got this one right?"

Richard's stomach turned on its end, and his throat closed for a second. A familiar chill shot down his spine again, and for the first time since he'd claimed Chamberlain's theories as his own, he feared that his time may have run out. *Did Chamberlain give him the wrong answer? Did he not hear it right and simply misrepresent the explanation as it was told to him?* Richard steadied himself and decided that brevity was the best policy.

"Yes, Dr. Branch. I do think I got this one right."

Branch had not yet looked up at Richard and the fact that he was not making eye contact threw Richard off what little game he had left. Branch was usually in total control of the room, but appeared now to be more confused than in command. He continued.

"I agree with you, Richard. I agree with everything you've said today, and I've agreed with everything you've said each time you've stood before us here. I agree so much with you that I must admit something to the team. I am confused. Explain something to me please. How is it that an intelligent young man like yourself, who should have never been at this company in the first place, can recover from your mistakes as remarkably as you do? And yes, I know about that. Quite impressive, by the way, how you snuck into the back of this room on the first day and stole that poor man's job. I knew all along. I gave you a chance because you risked something that day and that took guts. But guts aside, how is it that one day you make a disaster out of a customer meeting and the next day you hold the understanding of the business world in the palm of your hands? It does not add up to me. It's as if you are two different people. It's as if you have no belief in yourself and your abilities when you are in front of the customer and then twenty-four hours later you have the confidence of kings. I need to know how this happens, and I need to know now."

At this point, the other Client Executives and Branch himself were all leaning forward on their chairs with their elbows on the tables in front of them. They were waiting in sheer anticipation for Richard to reveal his secret like children eager to learn how the magician makes the massive elephant disappear. However, Richard was frozen in time. He did not expect this confrontation and was not prepared to speak. His mind was blank, and he was uncomfortable in the spotlight. Richard put his hands into his jacket pockets in an attempt to hide himself, and unexpectedly felt something gooey and wet on his right hand. He looked down as he pulled his hand from his coat pocket. When he opened his palm he smiled and every ounce of fear and concern melted away. In the middle of his hand was a chunk of an orange peel with teeth marks scored on its side. *Chamberlain.* Richard assumed that in Chamberlain's rush to consume the entire orange the day before, a small piece must have flown out of his mouth and somehow landed in Richard's pocket. The fact that Richard woke up late today and put on yesterday's clothes made him realize just how special his friendship with Chamberlain truly was. Chamberlain was here with him now, ready to help Richard save his job once again. Richard paused in deep thought as he reflected on how much Chamberlain had affected his life. He was so proud to call Chamberlain his friend. The old man was his mentor and savior, and deserved to be recognized for what he was: a man who suffered every day because of his past, but still held the truths of business in his grasp. So Richard clutched the orange rind in his hand and began to tell the story.

"Dr. Branch, you are right. It does not add up. It does not make sense that I can mess up so badly one day and then be able to speak like a professor at a business school the next, but I can because I am not alone. I am two people. Well, not me exactly, but there are two people. You see, after each mistake, I go to the subway across the street and talk to this homeless man. I feed him, and he helps me make sense of what I did wrong. We have become very close, and I am proud to call him my friend, but without him, I would not know what I did wrong. Without his help, you would have fired me a long time ago. So maybe I cheated. Maybe I used something available to me that others did not have access to. Maybe this man, this blessing of a man, maybe he's the one that you should hire. Maybe it should be him and not me here today with you."

Dr. Branch smiled suspiciously and said, "And Richard, what is this homeless man's name?"

"His name is Chamberlain Zacharias Taylor III."

With that, the entire room, including Dr. Branch, erupted in laughter. Everyone was cracking up at the insanity of this concocted story. No one believed Richard, but everyone just loved the fable. It was the first time that anyone had seen Branch laugh, and he was absolutely hysterical. He stood up, wiped the tears of laughter from his eyes, and walked over to Richard.

"Cast, you are one crazy S.O.B. What a story! Okay, look, if you want to keep it all a secret that's fine with me. Just keep doing what you are doing. You'll get it all squared away one day soon. I have faith in you. Oh! One last thing, Cast. You can keep your job again."

As Dr. Branch walked out of the room, his distant voice was heard fading down the hall as he said, "I go to the subway and talk to a homeless man. What a riot!"

Chapter 25

Cherise was cracking up as well. She had fallen to the floor laughing at the story. It was the funniest thing she'd heard in a long time, and it was all about her great-grandpa. She was so happy and alive despite the somber day. She was exactly how a little girl should be: carefree and full of life.

Cherise looked up from the floor and said, "So, they never believed you about my great-grandpa?"

"Nope. They thought I was making it all up."

"That is so funny, Mr. Richard."

"I know, Cherise. I was angry when it happened because they didn't believe me and because it felt like they were laughing at your great-grandfather, but it really was funny."

Cherise got back up, took Richard's hand and said, "So what happened next? Did you go see my great-grandpa again?"

"No. Not right away. I had one more meeting ahead of me."

With a hint of sarcasm, Cherise said, "Did you mess that one up too?"

"Hey! Give me some credit."

"I'm not trying to be mean, sir, but you do kind of make a lot of mistakes."

"I know I do, Cherise, but thanks to Chamberlain, I'm much smarter now."

The little girl smiled and said, "Keep going. I want to hear the rest of the story."

As Richard and Cherise made their way back to the front porch of the withered church, he continued to share his story.

****

ANALYSIS OF PRINCIPLE #4

You have to know who's cast in the play.

Unknowingly negotiating with someone who is not the final authority will likely result in your offering additional concessions when the ultimate decision maker arrives. This is such an important lesson to learn. Failure to qualify the person you are negotiating with before you make any demands or offer any concessions can have devastating results on the outcome of the negotiation. I cannot emphasize this point enough. As part of your negotiation preparation, you must seek to understand the roles that will be played by the people involved from both sides. You must know who from their side has the authority to say yes and can sign the contract. You must also know who will be involved on your side and what role you are being asked to play. If you enter into a negotiation without this understanding, you will end up giving away more than you bargained for, guaranteed.

So how do you determine if the other person has the authority to say yes? There are a few options available to you. First, you can do some research on your own. Searching the web, asking colleagues, or reviewing past contracts are just a few ways you can find out more about the other party. If you come up short with your research, your next best option is to ask the other person directly. Obviously, you need to handle this in a professional manner. You do not want to say, "Hey, are you the guy that can sign this contract or should I talk with your boss?" A question like that will do you no good, and will probably damage your chances of creating a lasting business relationship, let alone a mutually beneficial agreement. Even if the other person is not in a position of power today, he might get promoted next year, and if you've burned a bridge with him, it will be challenging to rebuild that relationship when he is in a position with more power. Remember to always treat others with respect regardless of title, position, or level of authority. Instead, be professional in your approach. You might say, "Before we begin, would you help me understand the signature process from your side so once we reach an agreement we can then move quickly through the paperwork?" Another respectful way to phrase the question is, "Will there be any other participants from your side that will need to approve what we've agreed to?" But never forget Chamberlain's Second Principle: ***"It takes a lot of bricks to build a house."*** You must be keenly aware that every position taken or demand made by the other party is only one element inside the complexity of a negotiation. Even if he responds that he has the authority to sign the contract, be prepared to have the rug pulled out from under you.

Sometimes the other party will say one thing and do another in order to gain an advantage in the negotiation. If you haven't experienced it yet, one day you will encounter a time when the person you are negotiating with claims to have signing authority only to reveal later that his boss needs to approve the agreement. This is a common negotiation tactic used to try to squeeze a little more out of the deal at the last minute, and that's why you never concede everything at your disposal. You never give everything away. Until that contract is signed, you never know if you're going to need to give away a little more to reach an agreement.

Going back to Richard's negotiation with Shilpa for a moment, we see that in addition to Richard's inexperience, his impatience was also a contributing factor to his error. Like many negotiators, Richard saw the finish line and rushed ahead in an attempt to make the sale. In Chapter 22, Shilpa gave Richard the green light to try to close the deal when she said, "Mr. Cast, I am quite impressed. You have made me feel very comfortable with your solution, and I would now like to draft the details of an agreement." She massaged his ego with her compliment, which distracted Richard from staying focused in the negotiation and he responded instinctually, not intelligently, when he jumped to his feet to grab the contract from the closet.

Let's pretend that through great questioning Richard discovered Shilpa was not the decision maker and confirmed that her father would need to approve the terms of the agreement before a purchase would be made. What should Richard do if Shilpa asks for a discount, free services, and free training? Should he stop negotiating all together and just deal with her father or is it acceptable to negotiate with the middle-man? The answer is, as it has been for most of the questions asked here, it depends. It depends upon what Richard and Dr. Branch have agreed to. It depends upon how many *X-Ray Now* systems Shilpa was planning to buy. It depends upon how much of a discount she asked for. It depends upon the true cost of the concessions to X-Ray Query, LLC. At this point in his career, the safest thing for Richard to do is ask to take a break so he can privately discuss the matter with Dr. Branch. Offering a concession here is unwarranted because Shilpa is not in a position to offer a commitment in return. Any promise she makes can be overridden by her father. So a concession here from Richard might be considered wasteful.

However, if Richard felt confident, he could test a potential concession or offer a conditional concession. In both cases, he would not be committing XRQ to anything concrete, nor would Shilpa be agreeing to something without her father's approval, but they could move the negotiation forward so they are closer to an agreement once the decision makers arrive. A potential concession test might sound like this: "If we offered free system support for one year, how might that influence your father's decision to move forward with the contract?" Again, the potential concession test is all about intention, not action or commitment. A conditional concession might sound like this: "If we offered a multi-unit price incentive, would you consider the purchase of more than one system?" As covered before, the conditional concession is a commitment. If I discount, will you buy? If Richard took the time to negotiate by using potential concession tests and conditional concessions, he might have been able to prepare an agreement in principle that Dr. Branch and Shilpa's father could have reviewed and finalized rather quickly.

As stated before, knowing who you are negotiating with and what his role is in the negotiation is critical to the success of the agreement. Act professionally here and never insult the other party if you determine that he does not have the authority required to close the deal. You never know where your career will take you, and he might end up being your boss one day, so be respectful to everyone involved in the negotiation, and always remember that ***you have to know who's cast in the play*** because unknowingly negotiating with someone who is not the final authority will likely result in your offering additional concessions when the ultimate decision maker arrives.
****

Chapter 26

The next day began poorly. Richard was disappointed to not find Chamberlain on the platform when he got off the train. He never knew where Chamberlain went, and it concerned him that something bad might have happened. The sky had turned dark, and it had unexpectedly started to rain. After crossing 8th Avenue, his suit was drenched, he had stepped in two puddles, one for each shoe, and his feet were swimming in pools of asphalt-infused pothole water. By the time Richard reached the office he was a soggy mess. He got an unsettling feeling that it was going to be a bad day. He was cold, depressed, and frankly in no mood for work.

Richard was still annoyed by the laughter and comments that Branch and his colleagues made the day before. He realized that his story about Chamberlain, although 100 percent true, sounded ridiculous, but when they laughed, it was like they were laughing at his mentor, and Chamberlain had no way of defending himself. Chamberlain had to unknowingly take their abuse and that angered Richard. How could he expect them to understand? They were clueless to the wisdom that Chamberlain shared with him. Clueless to the man that Chamberlain was, or where he came from, or how he fell so far from grace.

Richard sat in front of his computer quietly and waited for it to boot up. As he watched his monitor come to life, he began to question his own thoughts. *Who was Chamberlain really? He knew he was from North Carolina and that he once had a business and a family, but what else? Who was he? What really happened to him? How did he end up on the floor of the 8th Avenue and 34th Street subway?* Before Richard realized what his fingers were doing, he launched a web browser and typed "www.google.com."

As the familiar logo and text box appeared in the middle of the screen, Richard slowly typed the name "Chamberlain Zacharias Taylor III." The cursor blinked on and off just after the third "I" and Richard paused because he felt like he was doing something wrong. He felt like he was breaking into someone's house or reading someone's private journal without them knowing, but he wanted to know the truth, so he lifted his finger and clicked on the "Google Search" button. The massive search engine churned and went hunting for all possible matches. Just before the page refreshed with its findings, a hand came crashing down on his shoulder.

"Richard. In my office. We have to talk."

Richard whipped his head around just in time to catch Branch walking into his office. He jumped from his seat, wiped off as much water from his pants as he could, and followed Branch's orders. Out of respect for the expensive leather chair and for Dr. Branch himself, Richard chose to stand instead of plopping his wet body onto Branch's office furniture.

"Good morning, Dr. Branch."

"Good morning. You look like crap today, Richard. Got caught out in the rain, did you?"

Richard shrugged and said, "Yes. I wasn't expecting it to rain this morning. Would you like me to run home and change? Do we have a meeting today?"

"Actually, you have a meeting today. Fortunately for you, it's just a telephone call. So, no, I do not want you to run home. At least not before your call with Boopathi Subramanian at 7:30 a.m. They are ten-and-a-half hours ahead of us in Bangalore. It will be 6:00 p.m. there, and he will be just finished with his day. His daughter is in transit home. After you left, I sat down with Shilpa and asked her the exact question you stated in front of the room. I asked if it was Shilpa or her father who would make the final buying decision, and after a few minutes of posturing, she confessed that her father would have the final word. It was at that point that I removed the contract from the table and requested this conference call. Had you not figured out what mistake you made, I had every intention of taking this call myself, but I believe in you, Richard. You have a gift, but you don't trust yourself. You understand the art of negotiation better than many people I've met throughout my career, but you need to believe in yourself in order to achieve success. Now go get yourself cleaned up and come back to my office in thirty minutes to take the call from my desk."

Richard headed for the bathroom down the hall. He was depressed. Dr. Branch was right. Well, sort of right. Branch gave him more credit than he deserved, but he was dead-on regarding his lack of confidence. Richard felt defeated. If Chamberlain was not there to save him from falling, he would have been back at his family's convenience store long ago. Richard stood in front of the bathroom mirror for twenty minutes before he realized how long he had been staring into space. He was not ready for this call. He knew he was going to fail again. He just knew it. At one moment, Richard contemplated packing it all in, walking out the door, saying goodbye to Chamberlain one last time, and heading back to central Jersey, but he needed to finish what he started. He was on a journey and knew he needed to face his fears. With one final paper towel swipe across his shirt and pants, Richard headed back to Dr. Branch's office.

Chapter 27

As the phone connected across the world, Richard sat uncomfortably in Dr. Branch's executive chair while Branch stood behind him by the window. Richard took slow, even breaths and tried to calm his nerves. Then the ride began.

"Hello, this is Dr. Boopathi Subramanian."

"Good evening, Dr. Subramanian, this is Richard Cast calling from X-Ray Query, LLC in the United States. I understand that you are expecting my phone call. Is now still a good time for us to speak?"

"Why yes, young man. I am now relaxing at home with my lovely wife Deepti. How may I help you today?"

"Well, Dr. Subramanian, I had the pleasure of meeting your daughter the other day and was hoping to continue that conversation about our digital x-ray image solution."

"Ah yes, of course. Please do. Please do continue. My daughter told me such wonderful things. It all sounds quite interesting. Something we could certainly use here at our offices, but I would like to hear from you what you believe."

Richard hesitated for a moment and then asked, "What I believe? What exactly do you mean, Dr. Subramanian?"

"Well, son, I have been alive for a long time. I have watched my children grow into responsible adults. I have cared for many of my young grandchildren and throughout all my years, I have seen many ideas that look very attractive on the surface, but in reality, offer nothing more than just another way to do the same old thing. I would like you to tell me what you believe about your solution. I would like you to tell me if you believe my patients will receive better care from me if I own your system. I would like you to tell me what you truly believe, Mr. Cast."

Richard was lost. He had been well trained to articulate the value and benefits of the solution. He could successfully demonstrate the capabilities of the technology, but when it came down to it, he had never really given any thought to what he believed. Did he truly believe that *X-Ray Now* would impact the healthcare industry like the brochure said it would? So he paused and turned the chair to face Dr. Branch. Richard gestured with his hands to Branch as if asking, *"What do you want me to tell him?"* and Branch simply lifted his hand and pointed his finger right at Richard. Then, ever so gently, he turned his finger toward his own heart and touched it three times as if saying, *"Believe in yourself, trust your heart, and speak the truth."* Branch wanted Richard to tell the good doctor what he truly believed, and it was at that moment that Richard realized if he did not speak the truth and believe in what he was saying, he'd be making yet another mistake. Buyers know when they are being lied to or when the salesperson is just in it to make a quick buck. Buyers are savvy nowadays. They leverage the Internet to become informed consumers before making a purchase. Anyone in sales who denies this fact and tries to make his product or service sound better than it really is, or is unaware of how his offering compares to the competition's, will never have long-term success.

Richard suddenly understood that he must **build bridges with Truth, Honesty, and Integrity,** and if he truly believed in the merits and value of what he was selling, spoke from his heart, and always acted with integrity, his customers would trust that the concessions he offered throughout the negotiation would result in a fair and mutually beneficial agreement that would satisfy the interests of both parties.

Richard extended an open palm toward Dr. Branch, and the two men shook hands. There was a commitment and trust between them now that would not falter. Richard was going to be just fine, so he turned the chair back around, took a deep breath, and continued his conversation.

"Dr. Subramanian, I am very pleased that you asked me for my personal opinion and belief about our solution. I can speak from my heart and say with certainty that this technology is going to change the face of medicine as we know it. Your patients are concerned about one thing and one thing only: their health. When they are sick, they want the right answers fast, and they want to return to good health as quickly as possible. As a caring doctor, you want exactly the same thing, and in order to deliver that, you need accurate and instant answers to your own questions. You need information to be accessible twenty-four hours a day, three hundred sixty five days a year. You need seamless collaboration with experts who can lend their assistance, wherever they may be in the world. Nothing can stand in the way of you providing the best possible care for your patients, and Dr. Subramanian, that is exactly what we offer. Our solution delivers answers the moment you ask the question. *X-Ray Now* puts the power of information into your hands so you can help your patients live long and healthy lives. And Dr. Subramanian, I believe that's really what it's all about."

There was silence on the other end of the phone. Branch was up on his feet. Richard was sitting so far forward that he was about to fall off the front of the chair, and finally the good doctor from India spoke.

"Mr. Cast, please email the contract to my daughter Shilpa and we will sign it immediately."

"I certainly will, and I thank you so much for your time today."

"Son, my patients and I should be thanking you. I look forward to speaking with you soon."

"As do I, Dr. Subramanian. Thank you again."

"Good day."

"Good day."

Richard carefully placed the receiver into its cradle and turned around to face his boss. Dr. Branch was clapping his hands together in total admiration of his young pupil. Richard had knocked it out of the park, and Branch was blown away.

"WOW!!! Now that was absolutely perfect, Richard. I believe you have just crossed over to the other side. Excellent job. Absolutely an excellent job!"

Richard could not contain his emotions. He pumped a fist in the air and let out a Marine-like "Hoo-Ah!" He was feeling great and wanted to celebrate. Dr. Branch had the same idea.

"Richard, I have a call to make now. It should last about thirty minutes. Why don't you email Shilpa the contract and once I get off this call, I'll take you out for breakfast."

"Thank you, Dr. Branch."

Dr. Branch smiled and said, "Richard, today you get to call me 'Alan.'"

Richard nearly flew out of the office and headed back to his desk to email the contract over to India. Despite the fact that the day had started off so wet and nasty, Richard was in great spirits and felt like he was on top of the world, and then everything came crashing down as he stared at the heading of the first line on the Google search that had been waiting for his return. It read *"Chamberlain Zacharias Taylor III: How One Man Destroyed the*

Family Business & the Welfare of an Entire City."

As Richard's deflated body dropped into his seat, the blue hyperlink called out to him. He moved the cursor and clicked the mouse. Richard exhaled all the breath inside his lungs and said, "Oh, Chamberlain! What did you do?"

Chapter 28

Richard could not believe what he was reading. His mind raced and his heart crumbled. The article was from January 1958 out of a local Charlotte, North Carolina newspaper. Its description of Chamberlain and what he had done was difficult to read. The writer portrayed him as one of Charlotte's worst citizens in its history. He was called a traitor to his employees, an embarrassment to the economy, and a disappointment to his family. There was a picture of a young Chamberlain with his father and grandfather on either side of him. They had their arms around one another and were standing outside a very large textile factory. They all seemed so happy, but the caption below the picture read, *"Two years after his beloved father suddenly passed away, Chamberlain Zacharias Taylor III (center) singlehandedly destroyed the family business."*

Richard read on, but the article became more depressing line after line. There were so many families devastated by his mistakes. Then one sentence reached back and socked Richard in the gut. It was a quote from Chamberlain's young daughter Estelle. It said, *"My Poppa went away and Momma said she don't know if he's coming back. I don't know what he did wrong, but I miss him and want him to come home. He can come back and maybe get a new job so we can be happy again."*

Richard printed a copy of the article to show Chamberlain what he read. Richard needed to know if it was all true, and he wanted to ask Chamberlain to tell him the rest of the story. The newspaper could not be telling the truth. There had to be more to it. The article must have left something out. The Chamberlain that Richard knew was not capable of doing the things the article said he did, but if he did do them, there must have been a reason why. Richard pushed himself away from the computer, grabbed a copy of the article from the printer, and shoved it into his coat pocket. It was time to find Chamberlain. Richard ran to the elevator and hit the down button.

Just as the doors slid open, Dr. Branch came out of his office ready to share a celebratory breakfast with Richard. His entire demeanor changed when he saw Richard walking into the elevator. He called out, "Hey! Richard! Where are you going? What are you doing? I'm taking you to breakfast."

Richard looked back at Dr. Branch as he held the elevator door open with his hand. He lifted his head and called back down the hallway.

"I'm going to have to reschedule, Dr. Branch. I'm sorry. I have to find Chamberlain."

Richard jumped into the elevator and disappeared. As the doors closed, Dr. Branch thought to himself, "Who?" A confused Alan Branch turned toward his office, but stopped when Richard's computer screen caught his eye. He walked over, sat down, and began to read the article.

"Oh my God!"

****

<u>ANALYSIS OF PRINCIPLE #5</u>

Build bridges with Truth, Honesty, and Integrity.

If you truly believe in the merits and value of what you sell, speak from your heart, and always act with integrity, your customers will trust that the concessions you offer throughout the negotiation will result in a fair and mutually beneficial agreement that will satisfy the interests of both parties. At the heart of this principle lies one truth that is hard to deny: if you develop a relationship with the other party that is built on truth, honesty, integrity, trust and respect, you effectively create a framework that will help you overcome obstacles in the path of negotiating a mutually beneficial agreement. Obviously, there are never any guarantees that you will accomplish your goals, but by behaving in this positive manner, you give yourself the best possible chance to succeed. The sad commentary here is that all too often, negotiations are adversarial, and the parties involved do not seek to ensure the interests on both sides are satisfied. As someone who negotiates for a living, this saddens me because I know how much more can be achieved when both sides collaborate. So my hope and objective is to empower you with information that through practice you'll translate into knowledge that will result in many successful negotiations. But it all starts with you. If you support the notion that people want to do business with people that they know will treat them fairly, then there are factors within your control that will help you achieve negotiation success.

Let's explore the details behind the principle a bit further. When we say, "If you truly believe in the merits and value of what you sell, speak from your heart, and always act with integrity, your customers will trust that the concessions you offer throughout the negotiation will result in a fair and mutually beneficial agreement that will satisfy the interests of both parties," what does that really mean?

If you truly believe in the merits and value of what you sell: This is sometimes easier said than done. It's probably unrealistic to think that everyone believes 100 percent in the products and services they sell, but you should. Why would anyone be content in a job where he did not believe in the merits and value of what he was offering? I appreciate that we all have financial commitments in our lives that we strive to meet with the money we earn from our jobs, but that's not an excuse to sell something that you do not believe in or something you wouldn't buy. If you do not believe in the products and services you are selling, do you think that you are in a position to establish a trusted relationship with your customers? If you don't believe in what you are selling, but hawk its benefits to your customers, isn't that a form of deceit? And what lasting business relationship has ever been built on a foundation of lies? Understand that this is not a lecture encouraging you to quit your job. Rather, if you do not believe in the products and services you sell, challenge yourself or your employer to improve them for the purposes of creating more value to your customers. The more you believe in what you are selling, the more honest you'll be in the negotiation. And honesty leads to trusted relationships, which in turn leads to successful negotiations.

Speak from your heart: In other words, tell the truth. Never lie to the person with whom you are negotiating. This does not mean you should put yourself in a competitive disadvantage in the negotiation by exposing all your hidden objectives. Withholding information strategically is not the same as lying. When you speak from your heart, you offer honest information to the other party that he can use to make sound business decisions. When you speak from your heart, you never make false claims or promises and never misrepresent yourself or your offering.

Always act with integrity: Every salesperson has a quota to hit and is under some sort of pressure to make his number, but if you ever hope to build lasting business relationships that turn into repeat customers, you must always act with integrity. So, what does it mean to act with integrity? Simply put, acting with integrity means never doing, saying, or implying anything questionable for your personal or corporate gain that could damage the business at hand or any future business interaction with any potential customer.

Your customers will trust that the concessions you offer throughout the negotiation will result in a fair and mutually beneficial agreement that will satisfy the interests of both parties: If you have followed the guidelines above, then you are well on your way to building a relationship based on trust, and once you have that, you are one step closer to developing a mutually beneficial agreement. Going back to the opening comments again, the people you negotiate with are very much like yourself, and it's not unreasonable to think that most people would prefer to negotiate with someone who believes in their products, speaks truthfully, and acts with integrity. By behaving in this manner, collaborative negotiations can forge ahead and the give-and-take on both sides will be such that the interests of both parties have the best chance of being met. When there is trust between the parties negotiating, the concessions offered are generally more equitable than the concessions offered in an adversarial negotiation. Building solid business relationships, therefore, is critical to the success of the negotiation, and the fastest way to build a lasting business relationship is to believe in your products and services, speak truthfully at all times, and always act with integrity.

One underlying point here is the importance for you to believe in yourself and your ability to succeed as a negotiator. Trust that through your studies of the art of negotiating and your practice of the skills you've learned, you'll acquire the knowledge and experience needed to put you in the best possible position to navigate through your negotiations and reach the goal of creating a mutually beneficial agreement. As Richard discovered in Chapter 27 when he did some self-reflecting before sharing his true thoughts and feelings with Dr. Subramanian, it is important that you look in the mirror too. When you believe in yourself and in your abilities to negotiate collaboratively, success is not that hard. Have faith in yourself because if you truly believe in the merits and value of what you sell, speak from your heart, and always act with integrity, your customers will trust that the concessions you offer throughout the negotiation will result in a fair and mutually beneficial agreement that will satisfy the interests of both parties. And remember, to become a successful negotiator, you must **build bridges with Truth, Honesty, and Integrity.**

****

Chapter 29

Richard burst through the revolving door, stumbled outside onto the sidewalk, and was immediately hit with a wall of biting rain that had been falling since early that morning. He shielded his eyes and pushed through a crowd of people as he made his way over to the subway. A shrieking noise pierced the air and the gray sky seemed to flicker with hues of red and orange. As Richard waded through the flood that had consumed 8th Avenue, chaos and panic ran rampant at the vestibule of the subway. A massive fire engine and a battered ambulance were parked on the street, and their sirens blared as the lights on top of the vehicles spun around and around.

Richard jumped over a puddle and slipped on his way down to the platform below. Once inside the station and protected from the unforgiving elements above, life seemed to slow down as if everyone and everything was under water. There were EMTs scattered across the platform, while a few firefighters stood by taking charge of crowd control. Richard screamed.

"Chamberlain!"

He was waiting for his friend to echo back as they had done many times before, but despite all the commotion, there was only silence. He called again, but this time at the top of his lungs.

"CHAMBERLAIN!"

As if on cue, a sea of onlookers parted and created a pathway that led to the back wall where Chamberlain lay dead on the floor. Richard dropped to his knees and called once more, but his breath failed him and all that was heard was, "Cham..."

Richard pushed himself to his feet and ran to his friend. Chamberlain was dead. The EMTs had ripped his shirt open and tried resuscitating him with every means possible, but the old man's time had come. Richard knelt down next to his lost mentor and wept. He tried to take Chamberlain's hand, but one of the EMTs grabbed Richard's arm.

"Sir, please step away from the body."

Richard did not move. He was lost in time. This could not be happening. He had so many questions to ask Chamberlain. There were so many things left unsaid. Too many conversations not yet shared. Too many meals to buy. Too many lessons to learn. It was too soon. It was not fair. Richard looked up at the EMT and quietly spoke.

"His name was Chamberlain Zacharias Taylor III and he was my friend."

The EMT helped Richard to his feet and away from Chamberlain as the other emergency responders placed the body onto a gurney and began to wheel him away. Richard was dizzy and could not stand on his own. His head felt so light, and his legs buckled beneath him. As he dropped back to the floor where he had shared so much with Chamberlain, he called out to the EMT.

"Where are you taking him?"

As they pushed his mentor away, the EMT called back to Richard.

"We're headed to the morgue at Bellevue. You can view the deceased there."

And then they disappeared, as if Chamberlain had never even existed. He was gone and would never return. The crowd settled down and the normal comings and goings of people passed through the subway as Richard remained on the floor. When he finally looked at his watch, an hour had passed. Richard's legs were numb, and he just wanted to get to the morgue as fast as possible. He had no idea what he was going to do there, but he knew he had to see Chamberlain one last time. Richard tried to stand, but his legs had fallen asleep, and as he awkwardly fell to his side, his head hit something hard that resonated with a hollow thud.

Richard moved to his knees and rubbed his eyes. Lying there on the floor before him was Chamberlain's battered guitar. The three remaining strings had snapped and were dangling like long locks of hair. It had been pushed aside by the EMTs, and in Richard's daze he had not noticed it lying beside him the whole time. The crumbling guitar was face down on the cement, and as Richard pulled it toward him, he saw something that looked like writing on the back of it. The mangled letters looked like they had been scratched into the wood by a fingernail. The lines were crooked and some scores ran deeper than others.

Richard realized that he had never noticed the writing before because Chamberlain had always held that side against his body. He picked the guitar up as gently as he could, recalling how Chamberlain carefully ran his fingers along its wooden neck not so long ago. He read the inscription out loud.

"Above all, trust and believe in yourself."

Although Richard was already on the floor, his body sank deeper into the concrete. *"Above all, trust and believe in yourself."* That was the message of the lesson he learned during his call to India. The same message Branch had given to him earlier that day. *Did Chamberlain leave this inscription on the guitar for Richard? Impossible. How could that be? That made no sense. It must have been a message Chamberlain wrote to himself to remind him of who he was and where he'd come from, but the words touched Richard's heart.* Whatever it was, Richard imagined it to be the final piece of advice from his true friend. *"Above all, trust and believe in yourself."*

Richard took the guitar in his hands and held it close to his heart.

"Thank you, my friend. Thank you so much."

As Richard turned the guitar around, he heard a thud from inside the instrument and immediately remembered the orange that Chamberlain stashed away. He reached inside to pull it out, but what he touched did not feel like an orange. He thought it felt more like a book. Richard carefully held the object between his fingers and began to pull it out from the belly of the guitar. He turned his hand and out came a withered leather journal. Richard placed the guitar to the side and stared at the old book. Its cover was cracked and bent, and its pages were faded and brittle. He thought to himself, *"What in the world could this be?"* As he opened the leather cover to the first page, his heart skipped a beat as he read the first entry.

Dear Journal,

It is February 2, 1957. Poppa has been gone just over a year and today the IRS spent the afternoon with me. They say Poppa didn't pay all of his taxes for the past five years and that he did something they called embezzlement. I don't know what to believe, but they say things don't look good for the factory. What am I going to do? How am I supposed to save everyone?

Richard sat on the floor reading the journal for some time. He could not believe what had happened to his friend. One thing was certain. The tragedy that befell Chamberlain was not his fault, and he had done everything possible to save his business, his employees, and his family. The fact that Chamberlain carried his father's sins to his grave humbled Richard and made him appreciate Chamberlain more than ever before. As he closed the journal, Richard realized just how special Chamberlain truly was.

Chapter 30

Richard was surprised how quickly everything came together. He visited the morgue, identified the body, and placed a call to the Calvary Baptist Church in Charlotte, North Carolina. The article that Richard printed contained a handful of clues about how to contact Chamberlain's estranged family. A quick phone call to the 411 information operator led him to the church's number. Richard spoke with the pastor there, and was quickly put in touch with a woman named Estelle Taylor, Chamberlain's daughter.

It took more than fifteen minutes before Estelle stopped crying and praising the Lord, but when she settled down, she and Richard spent a good hour talking about her father and then worked out the details of the body transfer and funeral. Estelle's world had been ripped from her when she was just a child. She was forced to grow up without a father and had lived too many years in shame and public ridicule because of Chamberlain's devastating actions. For far too long, she had a hole in her heart where her father was supposed to be. She had grown cold and distant over the years, but no one could blame Estelle for turning out the way she did. Everyone in town knew it was not her fault. Although Estelle's emotions pulled her back and forth between anger and forgiveness, hate and love, she knew the closure that Richard was about to deliver was a true blessing. She was so touched by Richard's generosity and moved by his compassion that she resolved, as difficult as it was, to receive her father back with an open heart. Estelle was a 58-year-old loving mother and grandmother, but inside she was still that devastated little girl who never got the chance to kiss her poppa goodbye.

When they hung up the phone, they both sat alone and wept for this unforgettable man who had touched their lives. They would never be the same again.

Chapter 31

The sun had long since set and the moonlight filled the early evening sky. It was a clear night, and the stars shined brightly in the heavens. Richard looked down at Cherise as she sat with her face in her hands and cried. Cherise would also never be the same again for she too now knew Chamberlain.

"Cherise. Don't leave. I'll be right back. I have something for you."

Richard lifted himself from the steps and walked across the gravel parking lot to his rental car. He opened the back door and pulled out a large object wrapped inside a blanket. Cherise tried to see what Richard was doing, but there was not enough light, so she sat and waited and thought about her great-grandfather. Richard returned, sat beside the little girl, and placed the blanket on her lap.

"Go on, Cherise. Open it."

Cherise held the corner of the blanket and lifted it ever so slowly. As it fell to the side, the neck of Chamberlain's battered guitar glistened in the porch light. Her eyes grew large, and tears streamed down her precious little face. She pulled the blanket from the rest of the guitar and hugged it with all her might. She kissed it up and down and said over and over, "I love you, Great-Grandpa. I love you, Great-Grandpa. I love you, Great-Grandpa."

Richard leaned over and kissed Cherise on her head and stood once more.

"It's time for me to go now, Cherise. It was so nice to meet you today. Thank you for spending so much time with me. Your great-grandfather would have been very proud of you."

Cherise placed the guitar down on the porch and jumped into Richard's arms. She squeezed him tight and said, "Mr. Richard, thank you for bringing my great-grandpa home to my grandma. Even though she's so sad, I know you made her very happy. I like your story about Chamberlain a lot more than the ones I heard before."

Richard set Cherise back down on the porch and wiped a tear from her cheek. As he looked into her eyes, something told him that he'd see her again. He turned and slowly walked back to his car. The gravel crunched beneath his feet as he looked to the heavens and smiled.

"Thank you, Chamberlain. Thank you for everything."

Richard got in the car and drove off into the darkness.

The church doors opened and Estelle walked out onto the porch. She watched the dust trail settle along the dirt road as she lowered herself to the steps beside her granddaughter.

"Cherise, was that the nice young man?"

"Yes, Grandma."

"He's a good man, Cherise."

"Yes, he is, Grandma."

"What's that old guitar next to you, sweetie pie?"

With a twinkle in her eye, Cherise smiled and said, "That's you, Grandma."

"What's that, child? What do you mean, that's me?"

Cherise put her arm around her grandmother and said softly, "Let me tell you a story about a good man named Chamberlain."

Chapter 32

As Richard sat at the airport waiting to board his flight back to New York, he turned to the last page of the journal and read Chamberlain's final entry again.

January 27, 1958
Last night I went back to the factory and took this journal out of my desk. I will never let them know what Poppa did so I took this book with me. I never want them to know the truth. Poppa, you taught me everything I know. I miss you. I wish I could have been stronger for you. I hope one day everyone will find forgiveness in their heart for me. Until then, I will suffer along with those I failed to save. I love my wife. I love my daughter. Please watch over them for me. I will miss them terribly.

Richard closed the journal and made a silent promise that one day he would find a way to repay his friend. One day, Richard would set things right. Until then, he'd honor Chamberlain by perfecting the principles imparted to him.

****

FINAL THOUGHTS

Richard is well on his way to becoming an effective negotiator. He has acquired many skills during his time at X-Ray Query, LLC, and with Dr. Branch's support, Richard's career will flourish. He needs a lot more practice and will probably stumble along the way, but each mistake he makes will broaden his understanding of the art of negotiating. His ball of wax has begun to melt, and if he stays "tuned in" while negotiating, his solid foundation will serve him well.

What have you learned? Have you done like you were asked at the beginning and challenged yourself to think about negotiations differently than you have in the past? Has this validated principles you already knew? Did the story or the commentary on the principles make you realize something you had not thought of before? I hope the answer to these questions is "yes." There are hundreds, if not thousands, of negotiation principles, concepts, theories, and tactics, but the five presented here were specifically chosen because they range in scope from novice to professional, from tactical to strategic, and from logical to emotional. The broad scope of principles offers you the chance to rethink the way you approach negotiations, and your new way of thinking should help you achieve great success.

I'll offer two final comments that summarize my approach to negotiations. First, I believe that the only way to become an effective negotiator is to negotiate every chance you can. Never pass up an opportunity to hone your skills. Just having the information does not make you a negotiator. The information is critical to your success, but knowing how and when to use it is the objective. So study often, learn as much as you can, and then walk away from the books and sit down across the table from another human being and start talking. And that brings me to my second comment. A negotiation happens between two people. Please throw out that useless comment, "It's just business, it's not personal." Decisions may be made for business reasons, not personal ones, but you must always remember that there is a human being sitting in front of you and the decisions made in the negotiation will often times have a profound effect on you personally. You each have feelings, motivations, and beliefs that define who you are and influence how you interact with others. The more you seek to build a trusted relationship with the other person, the more successful you'll be at negotiating.

I'll end with this: Study hard, but practice harder. And never forget the principles that our dear friend Chamberlain has imparted to you here.

The Chamberlain Negotiation Principles

1. **A negotiation is a marathon, not a sprint**

2. **It takes a lot of bricks to build a house**

3. **Recognize when you are negotiating with gravity**

4. **Know who's cast in the play**

5. **Build bridges with Truth, Honesty, and Integrity**

****

The Chamberlain Negotiation Principles

Acknowledgments

Thank you to my family and friends who helped shape this book. Without your honesty, criticism, suggestions, and encouragement *The Chamberlain Negotiation Principles* would have never been possible. Thank you to Saul Kelner, Rhoda Schulman, Mort Schulman, David Richman, Marc Kelner, Corey Nathan, Cliff Ross, Phil Folz, Scott Budman, Al Vespoli, Sia Shalikar, Paul Shapses, Sue Shapses, Todd Brown, Rob Bardani, and Holly Stichka. Thank you to Chris Moran, Dan Whalen and Ellen Berlan for mentoring me and for teaching me about the art of negotiating. Thank you to my talented editor, Cynthia Sherwood (www.secondsetofeyes.com). Thank you to my creative cover artist, Wicked Sunny (www.publishinggurus.com). For all your love, thank you to the Silbersteins, the Schulmans, and the Kelners. A special thank you to my children, Coby and Tori, for always encouraging me to be the best I can be. And to my wife, Debbie, thank you for all your love and support.

Author Biography

Jared Kelner's career started in the mid 1990s in California where he opened a chain of secondhand children's clothing stores. *The Well Dressed Baby* was featured in the August 1998 issue of Entrepreneur Magazine in an article entitled "10 Best Children's Businesses You Can Start Now."

Since 1999, Jared Kelner has held several important service sales positions at one of the world's leading Internet corporations that designs and sells networking and communications technology.

In 2006, Jared started *The Infinite Mind Training Group* (www.memory-trainers.com), which offers interactive memory improvement training seminars to corporations and the general public.

Jared currently lives in central New Jersey with his wife and two children. To learn more about Jared Kelner, please visit www.jaredkelner.com.